sea_ice

sea_ice

FicSci 03

Edited by
Mehita Iqani and Wamuwi Mbao

AFRICAN
MINDS

Published in 2025 by African Minds
4 Eccleston Place, Somerset West, 7130, Cape Town, South Africa
info@africanminds.org.za | www.africanminds.org.za

The views expressed in this publication are those of the author. When quoting from any
of the chapters, readers are requested to acknowledge the author.

ISBN (paper): 978-1-0672536-5-3
eBook edition: 978-1-0672536-6-0
ePub edition: 978-1-0672536-7-7

Copies of this book are available for free download at: www.africanminds.org.za

ORDERS:
African Minds
Email: info@africanminds.org.za

To order printed books from outside Africa, please contact:
African Books Collective
PO Box 721, Oxford OX1 9EN, UK
Email: orders@africanbookscollective.com

Table of Contents

Acknowledgements

FicSci is a not-for-profit academic research project that aims to produce and support experimental interdisciplinary encounters between science and creative writing.

It is organised by the South African Research Chair in Science Communication and funded under the auspices of the National Research Foundation of South Africa.

FicSci is convened by Professor Mehita Iqani and Dr Wamuwi Mbao. For each workshop we invite a scientist specialist to share their research.

We are grateful to Dr Tokoloho Rampai for sharing her knowledge and time for FicSci 03.

Each workshop also invites select writers chosen through a competitive application process.

We thank all the writers who accepted our invitation and shared three days of their lives with us to participate in this bold experiment. We are grateful to all the writers for engaging with the post workshop process and for polishing their pieces based on our feedback.

We thank Fumani Jwara, Noxolo Mbazini and Elizabeth Newman for invaluable communications and logistical support on the project.

FicSci 03 was hosted at the Mont Fleur conference centre in the Blaauwklippen valley.

This anthology is available in its e-print version for free download to reach the widest audience. It is licensed under Creative Commons.

❄

Sea Ice Science

Tokoloho Rampai

Provocation 1: Research in/and the Antarctic

The Antarctic sea ice plays an important role in global climate and ocean systems; therefore, Antarctic sea ice is an important aspect regulating the response to and being impacted by anthropogenic climate change (Light et al., 2003). The structural properties of sea ice affect optical properties, the biology within the ice, the mechanical properties, exchanges between the atmosphere and the ocean, amongst other factors. The formation of sea ice affects other environmental systems and thermohaline circulation. Thus, studying the growth dynamics of sea ice and the resulting structure is of great importance.

Vast areas of silent, floating ice on frigid and uninviting seas, the polar regions have always been the subject of fascination and curiosity. The hostile climate has discouraged habitation and exploration of these regions, especially in the Southern Hemisphere, where the latitudes have become known by their tempestuous conditions, the roaring forties, furious fifties and screaming sixties (National Ocean and Atmospheric Administration [NOAA], 2017).

As exploration and knowledge of these regions has developed, scientists have come to realise the importance of sea ice.

The ice provides a barrier between the atmosphere above and the ocean below, affecting local and global climate, ocean mixed layer structure, and ocean heat flux (Brandon, Cottier and Nilsen, 2010; Morrison and Smith, 1981; Maykut and McPhee, 1995). The sea ice also provides a habitat for microorganisms that live within the brine channels present in the ice. Brines allow the microorganisms to access the light filtering in from above, while the nutrients they require are provided in concentrated doses from the ocean as the ice forms and rejects all impurities (Arrigo, Mock and Lizotte, 2010).

Considering the substantial role that sea ice plays in local and global climates, and its effect on radiative, heat and salt fluxes within the ocean, it is paramount that sea ice properties are studied and recorded. This is of special significance considering the impact of global warming upon the sea ice and the feedback that ice has on the climate system.

Original and independent sea ice research in South Africa started only recently (2017) thanks to a collaboration between oceanographers and chemical engineers at UCT. The first projects demonstrated the initial capability of carrying out research in Antarctic sea ice and were mostly focused on capacity building and community engagement for knowledge sharing.

For more see: Hall, B., Johnson, S., Thomas, M., and Rampai, T. "Review of the Design Considerations for the Laboratory Growth of Sea Ice", *Journal of Glaciology* 69, no. 276 (2023): 953–965. doi:10.1017/jog.2022.115

Provocation 2: Sea ice properties

Sea ice properties are also important for the environmental characterisation associated with shipping, offshore construction activities and tourism, which are increasing in the polar regions.

The safety and economic success of these endeavours depend on a comprehensive understanding of sea ice and its effect on these activities (Timco and Weeks, 2010). The polar regions are fragile environments, and the efforts to preserve them are continuing, especially in Antarctica, which is protected under the Antarctic Treaty of 1959, prohibiting commercial activities in the region and preserving it for scientific research (Secretariat of the Antarctic Treaty, 2011).

Timco and Weeks (2010) provide a comprehensive and thorough review of the engineering properties of sea ice, including mechanical properties such as tensile, uni-axial compression and multi-axial compression strength, elastic modulus and Poisson's ratio. It is important to note that all of the reviewed studies focus on Arctic ice and this study mostly spans from the 1960s to the mid-1980s. The mechanical properties of ice vary greatly, since they are a function of many factors including, but not limited to ice temperature, salinity and gas content, crystal size and orientation, load direction and strain rate (Schwarz and Weeks, 1977). In addition, the behaviour of ice shifts between inelastic and elastic, with viscoplastic behaviour also shown (Mellor, 1983). Therefore, there is a need for a compound model to describe the mechanical behaviour of sea ice, that aims to incorporate its different behaviour in different regions. These models can either be elastic-plastic or viscous-plastic (Feltham, 2008).

As input to these models, and for calibration purposes, the mechanical properties of ice need to be assessed under a variety of conditions and in laboratory experiments. The mechanical properties of interest and their current knowledge status are reviewed below. Elastic Modulus, or Young's Modulus, is the ratio of stress to strain during the elastic behaviour regime. Given a stress-strain curve, this can be obtained by computing the slope during the elastic behaviour; however, this is too impractical since it requires strain measurements from within the sample itself, not through the platens. The initial tangent modulus is constant for such a small region that it is difficult to obtain (Mellor, 1983).

For more see: Johnson, S., Audh, R.R., de Jager, W., et al. "Physical and morphological properties of first-year Antarctic sea ice in the spring marginal ice zone of the Atlantic-Indian sector". *Journal of Glaciology* 69, no. 277 (2023): 1351–1364. doi:10.1017/jog.2023.21

Provocation 3: Sea ice dynamics

Changes in salinity and temperature exert a fundamental control on sea ice physical, chemical and biological properties (Vancoppenolle et al., 2019). It is essential to have a deep understanding of desalination processes in sea ice, especially in the context of climate change, during which a substantial reduction in the sea ice extent is expected in both hemispheres (Comiso et al., 2017; Parkinson, 2019).

Previous observations have proposed that desalination of sea ice takes place through a variety of mechanisms during its growth and decay: for example, salt segregation at the growing ice-ocean interface, brine diffusion, brine expulsion, gravity drainage and flushing (Weeks and Ackley, 1986; Notz and Worster, 2009; and references therein). In growing sea ice, gravity drainage and salt segregation are thought to dominate desalination processes; the relative proportion of which remains hotly debated, as illustrated by the contrasting views in the conclusions of Notz and Worster (2009) and Middleton et al. (2016).

Gravity drainage refers to the draining of brines out of sea ice by convection caused by a hydrostatically unstable brine density profile. Brine density is primarily a function of brine salinity. Any temperature gradient in sea ice is accompanied by a salinity gradient in the interstitial brine to maintain phase equilibrium (Vancoppenolle et al., 2009). In growing sea ice, temperature decreases upward and, therefore, brine salinity increases upward: a configuration that is hydrostatically unstable. Depending on the permeability of the sea ice, this configuration may lead to convective overturning of brine and the replacement of some of the brine with the underlying seawater. The salinity difference between the brine leaving sea ice and the brine entering sea ice is the cause for the net desalination by gravity drainage (Eide and Martin, 1979; Notz and Worster, 2009).

Observations in both field and controlled-lab experiments have highlighted the key role of brine channels as a major path for brine rejection in growing sea ice (Wakatsuchi and Kawamura, 1987; Eide and Martin, 1975; Cole and Shapiro, 1998; Cottier et al., 1999; Middleton et al., 2016). However, there are still unknowns regarding the nature of brine overturning (i.e., on-off behaviour, onset development, etc.) and its relationship to internal ice microstructures (i.e., meandering of brine channels, roles played by ice crystal lamellae, etc.).

Salt segregation at the growing ice-ocean interface refers to a process by which most of the salts are rejected from the newly growing pure ice crystals and become concentrated at the interfacial boundary layer between the ice and the ocean (Weeks and Ackley, 1986). By itself, the morphology of the ice-ocean interface (i.e., 'the skeletal layer') requires that this process occurs. The segregation of salt at the interfacial boundary layer leads to a diffusion of salt away from this interface. In parallel, the freezing point decreases with increasing salinity, as an increase in salt concentration goes along with a drop in temperature. Different rates between the transport of heat and salt diffusion leads to the development of a constitutionally super-cooled layer at the growing interface (Weeks and Ackley, 1986; Petrich and Eicken, 2016).

Any small perturbation from the planar growing interface, protruding in the constitutionally super-cooled layer, has a growth advantage and explains the lamellar structure of the interface: consisting of sub-millimetre-thick blades of ice separated by narrow films of brine. The presence of this interfacial boundary layer is required to explain many of the chemical fractionation processes that are observed in growing sea ice, such as the fractionation of gases (Tison et al., 2002). This statement relies on Tison et al.'s (2002) observations of the continuous bulk salinity field across the ice-ocean interface with no immediate segregation of salt at the advancing front. The observation of continuous interfacial convection by Middleton et al. (2016), independent of the location of brine channels, contradicts this statement. However, except for Middleton et al. (2016), these imaging methods suffer from the important drawback that internal structures in the ice can only be investigated after growth in 'post-mortem' investigation.

For more see: Moos, S., Rampai, T., Vichi, M., Tison, J. L., De Witt, A., and Fripiat, F. "Investigating the dynamics and exchanges across the ice-ocean interface in artificial sea ice". South African National Antarctic Programme, 2024.

References

Arrigo, K. R., Mock, T. and Lizotte, M. P. "Primary Producers and Sea Ice", in Thomas, D. N. and Dieckmann, G. (eds) *Sea Ice.* 2nd edn. Wiley-Blackwell, 2010.

Brandon, M. A., Cottier, F. R. and Nilsen, F. "Sea Ice and Oceanography", in Thomas, D. N. and Dieckmann, G. (eds) *Sea Ice.* 2nd edn. Wiley-Blackwell, pp. 79–110, 2010.

Comiso et al., "Variability and Trends in the Arctic Sea Ice Cover: Results From Different Techniques", *Journal of Geophysical Research Oceans* 122, (2017): 6883–6900.

Eide, L. I. and Martin, S. "The Formation of Brine Drainage Features in Young Sea Ice", *Journal of Glaciology*, 14, no. 70(1975): 137–154.

Feltham, D. L. "Sea Ice Rheology", *Annual Review of Fluid Mechanics* 40 (2008): 91–112. doi: 10.1146/annurev. fluid.40.111406.102151.

Feltham, D. L., Untersteiner, N., Wettlaufer, J. S. and Worster, M. G. "Sea Ice is a Mushy Layer", *Geophysical Research Letters* 33, no. 14 (2006): 4–7. doi: 10.1029/2006GL026290.

Feltham, D. L. and Worster, M. G. "Flow-Induced Morphological Instability of a Mushy Layer", *Journal of Fluid Mechanics*, 391 (1999): 337–357.

Feltham, D. L., Worster, M. G. and Wettlaufer, J. S. "The Influence of Ocean Flow on Newly Forming Sea Ice", *Journal of Geophysical Research* 107, no. C2 (2002): 3009. doi: 10.1029/2000JC000559.

Maykut, G. A. and McPhee, M. G. "Solar Heating Of The Arctic Mixed Layer", *Journal of Geophysical Research* 100, no. C12 (1995): 24691.

Mellor, M. "Mechanical Behavior of Sea Ice", *Cold Regions Research & Engineering Laboratory*, 1983: doi: 10.1007/978-1-4899-5352-0_3.

Middleton, C. A., Thomas, C., De Wit, A. and Tison, J.-L. "Visualizing Brine Channel Development and Convective Processes During Artificial Sea-ice Growth Using Schlieren Optical Method", *Journal of Glaciology* 62, no. 231 (2016): 1–17.

Morrison, J. and Smith, J. D. "Seasonal Variations In The Upper Arctic Ocean As Observed At T-3", *Geophysical Research Letters* 8, no. 7 (1981): 753–756.

National Ocean and Atmospheric Administration. "What Are The Roaring Forties?" *National Ocean Service.* 2017. Available at: htttps://oceanservice.noaa.gov/facts/roaring-forties.html.

Notz, D. and Worster, M. G. "Desalination Processes of Sea Ice Revisited", *Journal of Geophysical Research* 114, no. 5 (2009): 1–10. doi: 10.1029/2008JC004885.

Parkinson, C. L. "A 40-y Record Reveals Gradual Antarctic Sea Ice Increases Followed By Decreases At Rates Far Exceeding The Rates Seen In The Arctic", *Proceedings of National Academic of Science* 116, no. 29 (2019): 14414–14423.

Petrich, C. and Eicken, H. "Overview Of Sea Ice Growth And Properties". In David N. Thomas (ed.), *Sea Ice,* Wiley Blackwell, 1–41, 2016.

Schwarz, J., Frederking, R. M. W., Gavrillo, V., Petro, I. G., Hirayama, K. I., Mellor, M., Tryde, P. and Vaudrey, K. D. "Standardized Testing Methods for Measuring Mechanical Properties of Ice", *Cold Regions Science and Technology* 4 (1981): 245–253.

Schwarz, J. and Weeks, W. F. "Engineering Properties of Sea Ice", *Journal of Glaciology* 19, no, 81 (1977): 499–529.

Secretariat of the Antarctic Treaty. *The Antarctic Treaty.* 2011. Available at: www.ats.aq/e/ats.htm.

Timco, G. W. and Weeks, W. F. "A Review of the Engineering Properties of Sea Ice", *Cold Regions Science and Technology* 60, no. 2 (2010): 107–129. doi: 10.1016/j.coldregions.2009.10.003.

Tison et al. "Tank Study Of Physico-chemical Controls On Gas Content And Composition During Growth Of Young Sea Ice", *Journal of Glaciology* 48 (2002): 267–278.

Vancoppenolle, M. et al. "Role Of Sea Ice In Global Biogeochemical Cycles: Emerging Views and Challenges", *Quaternary Science Reviews* 79 (2013): 207–230.

Vancoppenolle, M. et al. "Thermodynamics of Sea Ice Phase Composition Revisited", *Journal of Geophysical Research* 124 (2019): 615–634.

Wakatsuchi, M. "Brine Exclusion Process From Growing Sea Ice", *Contributions From The Institute of Low Temperature Science* A33 (1984): 29–65.

Wakatsuchi, M. and Kawamura, T. "Formation Processes of Brine Drainage Channels in Sea Ice", *Journal of Geophysical Research* 92, no. C7 (1987): 7195–7197. doi: 10.1029/jc092ic07p07195

Weeks, W. F. and Ackley, F. "The Growth, Structure and Properties of Sea Ice". In N. Understeiner (ed.), *The Geophysics of Sea Ice*, Plenum, pp. 9–164, 1986. doi: 10.1007/978-1-4899-5352-0_2.

Weeks, W. F. and Cox, G. F. N. "Laboratory Preparation of Artificial Sea and Salt Ice", *Cold Regions Research & Engineering Laboratory,* 1974.

1

Pancakes

Wamuwi Mbao

We don't think of ice as wilderness. The wild is overgrown. Verdant. Warm. The Antarctic doesn't fit with this way of seeing things: its materiality appears glassy, closed off. The newspapers report that the amount of Southern Ocean that freezes over is shrinking. It's difficult to make this point stick. Ice disappearing from the Antarctic is not believable behaviour at all. We hold it at arm's length. If the ice is not where we are, it can remain in the abstract. We have a long history of holding the icy places at a distance: we imagine them as white places to be explored only by the intrepidly white. In older times, the great problem that had to be tackled was an abundance of ice. Ships playing the economies of their day (whaling, mostly, but also exploration) had to contend with vast fields of sea ice. The melting is a kind of reorganising of the world.

***

Scientists are trying to understand why the sea ice is breaking up at the rate that it is. They are trying to figure out what the melting ice will mean. The consequences are outside the frame for the time being (outside your frame: you use a different frame to the scientists). There are suggestions that, for a host of reasons, we need to submit the ice to surveillance, because the ice that is going away won't be coming back. We have learned that there are different kinds of ice. Grease ice. Pancake ice. Ice pans. Scientists are constantly touching, poking, prodding at ice and hoisting it, placing it in tanks and exposing it to waves. The work of categorising ice, making its states and conditions knowable, making its movements readable, is taking place as you're reading this sentence. In this regard, scientists are taking their explanatory framework from the explorers of the past.

***

Animated conversation, indistinct chatter
"You can play the odds."
"How long have you been here?"
"It happened because of an atmospheric river."
"I'll be here until Sunday."
"They're just for the look—they're not prescription."
"Do you want ice with yours?" *laughter*
"We, the unwilling ..."
"Do you know when this starts?"
"That's him over there."
"I had this dream last night ..."
"Does Ice Speak?"
"Did you apply?"
"Ice creeps while you sleep."
"I can't read my writing."
"I read that a piece of ice the size of Pretoria broke off."

***

The sound of frozen water undoing itself is rhythmic. Drip. Lap. Clack. Squeak. Nails on a distant chalkboard. Roars and whistles and wails that plunge and pour forth. The sonic landscape gives way to sudden craters of silence. Researchers bury receptors in the ice, and these receptors produce evidence of the ongoing noise. They hope, so they say, to use this noise as evidence that things are happening out there. Wild ice is very different to the domestic ice that clinks mutedly in your glass.

***

One brings a guitar. One wears a beard. One has a nervous laugh. Twenty-five past. They gather in the room that is shaped like a jar, and they chat amongst themselves as they wait to hear what they have been selected to do. Over four days, personalities thaw. Conversation lassoes itself to the weather, to writing, to the lives that have been left in other towns, other cities, shared or distant. There is a need for conviviality before what we do not know.

***

The shift wherein ice became, not an impediment to economic journeying, but an object whose wellbeing was a source of existential concern, reflects a late-stage worry about impending apocalypse.

In the morning, at breakfast one sits alone. Three share a joke. After the meal, three go forth, and two remain behind. Two sit by the fire. "It's how we make sense of the world," one says. One says, "Where is the link?" It will be a day of questions. It's not warm enough, in the board room, outside the room, everywhere on the hillside. Too cold for a t-shirt, too hot for a sweater. The day is reserved for discussions about thermal relationships. What are we meant to do with this information? The abstractness encourages dissociation. Nobody asks what it smells like, all that ice. At tea-time, discussion clusters form. One returns to the board room. Three decamp, taking their conversation with them.

***

It rains and it rains, and the sky is grey. The road down from the mountain retreat is briefly blocked. Should we be worrying when there's so much rain? Water is a commodity with its own agency, whatever form it chooses to take. We can't contain it indefinitely.

011

Our extractive relationship to water threatens to be redrawn along undesirable lines. What will the future look like? Whose future? In the presentations, the Antarctic territories seem to figure as an unpopulated icescape. The icescape has been gradually encroached upon by meaning-infrastructures from places invested in securing the continuity of certain ways of living. For those who do not belong (or belong only peripherally) to the socialities that are beginning to crumble and fray at the edges under climate change, the changes are not good.

***

Ice seems to look the same everywhere. This makes it convenient for representing climate disaster in a very general way. You've seen the scenes before. Ice sheering off glacier cliffs and sliding into the sea. Lonely polar bears. That kind of thing. Don't pity the animals. More than 90% of all the animals that have ever lived are now extinct, MOST OF THEM UNREMEMBERED. There is, some feel, still time for knowledge to become practice. There is still a sense that this story is bigger than us, out of human scale.

2

The History of Ice

Efemia Chela

I could tell you that I think in PSUs and atmospheric ice nucleation. I could tell you I have an optimistic disposition. I could tell you how I work interdisciplinarily, multidisciplinarily, even transdisciplinarily. I could tell you of the many times microcrystals have speckled my gloves and algae has clung to the spikes of my boots during sample collection. I could tell you about the bitter spring in the marginal ice zone. I could tell you about Stefan's Law. I could tell you about the history of sea ice. But I am running out of time.

I want to tell—

Since a noise outside my porthole's distracted me, I'll take you along on my investigation. Watch me pull on my boots and stuff my curly hair into a balaclava. I pick up my storm lamp and follow what sounds like ... Laughter? Crying? Chatter? The wind feels like about 39km/h and it rinses my tear ducts colder than you can imagine. No one's meant to be outside right now. Most people would not want to. Scientists, however, are not most people by nature. I turn on my headlamp and look over at the scales of ice rising and falling. Some say the ice creaks and cracks like an old chair. Others say it whinnies like a white horse. My ex-wife heard only whispers and screams. To me, it sings a curious and joyful song. I stop to listen to it for a moment, even though the cold shatters my knees.

I walk towards the shape near the ship's bow. It's Frans with his blue beanie, intent on something in his hands. Frans makes sure to scowl whenever I approach him, to counteract my cheerfulness. Some people think us seafolk should be dour, but I am happiest in my thermal layers, coring into ice. Frans always takes ladders two rungs at a time and the first thing he said to me on the SA Sarah Baartman was "There are no friends on the ice." I'll win him over. He is whittling a chunk of ice delicately and patiently. Anger hijacks my hands before I can stop myself. I can be overprotective of the ice. *Plop!* He glares at me as I storm off. I'd send him back to land if I could, but at the 60th parallel south we're too far off the continent.

We are thick and thin, and fragile and porous. We control the migration of birds, the appetites of mammals. We shred ships. We slip on the surface of the water.

Day is four hours long; night, five times that. Night and day don't matter when we work; the ice is a patient model. The twin meteorologists ring the bell when conditions are perfect, and we go out into the breach. Once, they broke protocol and we suited up to see a 10-foot swell, frozen in a majestic curve. I issued some fines, government rules, it's taxpayers' money after all, but forgave them onshore. Some shifts are fourteen hours of heavy lifting and painstaking, slippery work. The Antarctic doesn't make things easy, and I'm in love with its complexity.

I want to tell you about the silver-toned light—

"Polar Engineer Bruce?"

The electro tech looks at the men around me, they often do in the first week. I giggle at the mistake and wave. I inspect the sensors the electrical team have been fine-tuning for us to leave behind when we return to land. Five of them are good to go. I send the rest back. The tech looks disheartened, but I assure her she'll have another set up to spec by tomorrow.

At sea, the 4 hours of daylight screws up my circadian rhythm. While I spend the night hours reading, my mind casts back, "What was Frans carving?".

We need imperfections to form. We grow from the top down.
We are well-seasoned. We are proud of our mushy layer.
We are the bottom of the world.

I want to tell you how we started with nothing but a cut up Jojo tank tied to the roof of my car and a grad student who was figuring out his meds and our coding. I want to tell you that things in nature tend towards low energy. I want to tell you about my second sight: the inventions I envisage before others can. I want to tell you that salt depresses the freezing point of seawater. I want to tell you—

But as Narcissus had his pond; I have the inbox, the reflecting pool of the soul. Mine is always bursting.

The desalination exec who wants scoops on my new discoveries usually starts his emails with "Hey baby" and ends with an offer of preferential shares. He calls me his favourite, but I know he has a scientist at every pole. I respond with some cute selfies I took with the usual NDAs.

A shipping magnate and the minister of agriculture are embroiled in a long thread spooling over months. They want to know how fast the sea ice is going to melt in one concrete figure. I'm drawing it out with explanations of the science. I don't think they'd like the long equation that explains it better than one number ever could. I'll get back to that another day.

An eight-year-old from Canada asks, "Does pancake ice tastes like pancakes?" I write back that it does and if he does well in science, he's welcome to come around and taste it for himself.

The atmosphere here usually tastes like salt and smells like diesel, until you leave the ship. Then out on the ice it smells clean as a fresh ream of paper or like absolutely nothing at all.

We are columnar. We are granular. We are a viscous liquid.
We relish disturbance. We are the shining landscape.

Interviewers and friends are always concerned with what I'm missing (fyi: my Burmese shepherd and cheese—which has a better texture on land) as much as my achievements. First black woman commandeering an Antarctic mission. Inventor of thermal microtome procedures for cutting artificial ice. Disproving existing theories on the rate of surface energy transfer. They all just want to know what I miss when I'm at sea. I laugh and say the beach. If I was honest, I would say I miss the lab most of all. Its serenity, its limitless potential, the Belgian chocolate hidden behind the beakers at my station.

I am watching two students play table tennis on the deck, but I want to tell you about the day he came to the lab. I was fiddling with salinity ratios in the 500ℓ water troughs which were far too high. Sakaria came to build the flume machine so we could make waves indoors, agitate saltwater and replicate the ice we find in the field. He measured the space, cut the glass, smoothed out my pencil sketches with calloused hands and squared off fingertips. The wings of sandpipers fluttered in my stomach.

I had given the students the weekend off. Hileni, my deputy, was in the gym, focusing on her strength training for our next expedition. We were alone amongst the equipment, and I had been playing some Brubeck to keep us company. Sakaria was hammering and intermittently humming along. When the album started over, he asked me for a dance. We held each other close as the edges of the evening softened. "It's too late to work," he whispered. I removed my white coat, and he, his overalls. When we were totally naked, I led him to knowledge, like Eve did Adam. I lay down in drinking trough A, afloat on my back. He lay down in drinking trough B. "What's happening?" he panicked. "It's 30 per cent sodium chloride, baby," I purred. We held hands over the brim.

> *We have algae hiding in our brine channels. We are born of the first crystal in autumn and winter. We die more each summer. We act like concrete. We are glad to see you again, Dr.*

Today we have to core through the ice and extract samples for testing. I look forward to the physical work, a break from the mental strain. I put on all my layers and go out onto the deck. My glaciology students are sweeping the snow with the deck broom hung up by the door. I was awake but didn't hear it fall in my cabin. I do a head count and find Oko is missing. She must have overslept or still be seasick. I never manage to reach that liminal mental hallway between wakefulness and sleeping. I can't afford it. But sometimes I see the gleam of it in the support staff's faces a couple of weeks into our journey to the known world's end, and smile at their peaceful haze.

We sailed into a perfect quadrant of pancake ice and the captain woke me up blasting 'She Blinded Me with Science' into my cabin (I got tired of 'Ice Ice Baby'). I have instructed team one to lift whole pancakes onto the ship for study. While team two is being lowered into a pod with me to sail out. As the orange boat riffles the lenses of ice, it is tempting to dip your fingers in the water, but safety first. Hileni is on board, binoculars out, hoping to catch some of her beloved birds. So far, the blue-eyed shag has evaded her. What my best friend lacks in work ethic, she makes up for in loyalty.

The ice acts differently under a layer of snow. In fact, the far field ocean, 200m below the surface, is warmer than people think. Relatively. Thérèse, the slightly older meteorologist with broken red capillaries bringing out the wistful green of her eyes, slipped the report under my door this morning. I raced to catch her and ask for news of any potential storms. Every look she gives me denies she's gotten into the ethanol drum. "Perfect conditions. No storms predicted," she says. We'll help her on shore.

It's minus eighteen degrees today. The air is the coldest thing in the Antarctic. I watch my best student, Kehinde, forget this when his pincer tool slips and drops into the water. He whips off his glove and plunges it into the water. Reflexes can kill you on the ice. In a second, his hand is out again, being gnawed by the wind chill. Pride in his nimbleness warps into horrible pain. His fingers are already bulbous and blue. I drop the electromagnetic drill and stuff his hand under his armpit as he weeps. I send him back to the ship on the motorboat. They'll come back for us. Right now, we need to keep coring the ice that brought us all here.

We are on a freeze and melt cycle. We are under-researched.
We can be grease, nilas and frazil ice. We are part of the
largest natural seasonal event in the world. We feel her take
us away and promise to give back to us.

Our work is done. We're sailing back home. It's party time! The chef is conjuring up a feast with more sugar, cream and carbs than we usually get. On the last trip, the Russians smuggled aboard some caviar. To say there's better funding in the global north is an understatement. Thérèse is in the sick bay with mild alcohol poisoning. Kehinde has his arm in a sling. To *gbeku* on the dancefloor you only need one hand and two vibrating hips, so he's in luck. And these are the lowest injury numbers on an expedition in two years! The insurers will be delighted. Shea is glued to the football on the flatscreen, trying to see her family in the stands. The captain is rapping, very off beat. The interns are loving it anyway. Hileni and Frans are smiling too much at each other, talking about sheathbills and Adélie penguins. I wonder where I put those relationship disclosure forms? We might need them for next year's trip. *Stop planning and have fun,* I tell myself. Before I give my homegoing speech, I step out for some air.

I look out into the dark, unable to see much. But I know in the distance is the landfast ice, and beyond it lies the land. No matter how much I love this work—the comforting sound of the ship groaning and listing, screaming into the rushing Antarctic wind that steals my voice and thins it into silence, my precious ice that must be saved—something in the human spirit always recognises the shore as salvation.

3

Verweer

Emile Cronje

11 Junie 2032 — Siekeboeg
Wanneer Karin bykom, staan die hele span rondom haar. Sy knip haar oë 'n paar keer, en die wêreld kom stadig in fokus. Tlhologelo staan by haar regterskouer, 'n diep frons op haar gesig gekerf.

"Karin, can you hear me?" vra sy. Karin se oë val toe, en sy val terug in die donker binne haar.

"K-bear!" Met moeite sleep sy haar oë weer oop. Knik stadig.

"Yebo, Dr T." Haar stem kraak, herinner haar aan die geluid van die ys wat meegee onder haar.

"What were you thinking?" begin Mel, maar Tlhologelo maak hom stil.

"Let her rest first, Mel." Sy druk saggies Karin se hand en verstel die kussing agter haar kop.

"We're really glad we saw you in time," sê sy. Karin gee 'n effense glimlag. Sy is nie seker dat sy bly is om wakker te word nie.

Onder die water. Sneeupak word swaarder en swaarder. Sink. Die diepte maak alles stil, selfs die stemme wat gewoonlik nooit ophou skree nie. Hoor hart klop; stadiger en stadiger soos wat die donker nader kom.

Die eerste keer wat sy 'n timelapse van die ysbank rondom Antarktika gesien het, was sy 'n jong student. Haar dosent—Dr Simelane, die eerste vrou aan wie sy skelm liefdesbriewe geskryf het—was besig om te verduidelik:

019

"If rainforests are the lungs of the earth, the formation and melting of sea ice is the heartbeat. This process drives the global thermo-haline circulation, maintaining our oceans' currents. Added to that, the change in saline concentration that results from the dynamics of the ice's formation also stimulates the food chain. Because ice crystals push out impurities as they form, the water directly underneath a forming ice shelf is flooded with salty rivulets, which you can see in this video here ..."

Met 'n laser-pointer op die skerm gemik, het daar diep kuiltjies in Dr. Simelane se wange gekeep wanneer sy vir die klas glimlag.

"These brine channels within the ice provide a home for algae, the growth of which of course creates another entry into the food chain. When summer comes and the ice melts, not only does the salinity drop; the algae is also released back into the ocean, taking away their refuge and making them easier to consume. A kind of spring bloom, if you will, giving new life to the cold ocean."

Sak dieper, hartklop en ys pols saam. Binnewêreld omarm die wêreld buite—elke storm, elke misdaad, elke bom. Elke verraad, elke liefde, elke blom. 'n Prisma plooi oop, en 'n stem roep: "Weerenweerverweer. Weer verweef, verteer, verskeur, verweer. Kom terug. Kom weer."

12 Junie 2032 — Kajuit

Wanneer haar oë weer oopgaan, is dit net Mel in die siekeboeg saam met haar. Hy lê in 'n stoel en slaap. Sy kop is ongemaklik teen sy skouer gekantel. Sy skuifel haar bene tot op die rand van die bed en laat sak haar voete stadig. Haar kop begin onmiddellik draai, en sy trek haar asem skerp in. Mel word wakker en storm na haar sy.

"You're such a hazard to yourself, you know that?" Sy glimlag swak en steek haar hand uit. Sy uitdrukking versag en hy kom sit langs haar.

"I thought I ... I though we had lost you." Sy weet nie hoe om vir hom te sê dat sy meer verlore voel as ooit nie. Sy druk sy hand saggies. Hy raak teer aan haar wang, sy sien hy is bang.

"Karin, did you ...?"

"Mel, I heard something speak to me. While I was unconscious."

"Like a dream, you mean?" Sy frons. Was dit net 'n droom?

"I don't think so," antwoord sy. "There was something ... clear about it."

"A lucid dream, then."

"No! It pulled me back, Mel! It pulled me back, and I didn't ..." Haar stem raak weg. *Ek wou nie terugkom nie*, erken sy aan haarself.

Heelwat later, wanneer sy uiteindelik alleen is, skribbel sy die stem se woorde in haar dagboek:

Weer en weer verweer.
Weer verweef, verteer
en verskeur,
meer verweer.

Kom terug.

Kom weer.
Jy groei, ek gee.

***

Sy het weke lank gewag op 'n geleentheid om te spring. Te val. Te verdrink. Maar daar was altyd iemand op die dek. Die skip gaan net aan wal wanneer die hele span dit moet verlaat. Almal hou mekaar altyd in die oog. Sy het langer en langer ure net buite gesit en die verskil tussen die uitgestrekte wit en die geskarrel rondom haar ingeneem. Thlologelo sou nou en dan opdaag met 'n stomende koppie—tee, of gemmer, of polisiekoffie. Kort, bekommerde gesprekke.

"When was the last time you spotted a whale, K-bear?"

"Perhaps two years ago, T."

"I wonder where they're playing this season."

"I'm not sure they have the energy." Sy wil nie hardop sê dat hulle waarskynlik besig is om van die honger te vrek nie.

"T ... What's your biggest fear?" vra sy een dag. Die soekende blik van haar spanleier is op haar gefokus, haar kollega, haar rots. 'n Lang teug aan 'n beker. Êrens roep 'n albatros.

021

"I don't know … Probably hurting someone I care about without intending to." Skaamheid. Wegkyk.

"And yours?"

"Living forever."

***

26 Junie 2032 — Laboratorium

Sy mag nie meer veldwerk doen nie. In die laboratorium herhaal sy analises—onnodig, nie volgens protokol nie—op soek na iets waaraan sy nie 'n naam kan gee nie. Veertig CT's van dieselfde monster. Sy maak die eerste een oop. Kleure spoel oor mekaar—water, silt, gapings, alge. Sy bestudeer die volgende een, beweeg heen en weer tussen die twee. Dieselfde kleure, dieselfde gate. Derde, vierde. Een van die spatsels blom. Dit is te verwagte. Vyf, ses, sewe—groter en groter soos wat die ys smelt. Agt, nege … Die spatsel krimp. Karin hou op. Begin weer voor. Daar is dit weer: 'n kol alge groei en krimp, groei en krimp. Sy blaai deur veertig monsters —*Jy groei, ek gee …* Sy hou op, begin weer aan die begin. Mel stap in.

"What are you doing?" Sy draai verward om.

"Nothing. Looking at images."

"Show me?"

Sy wil nie.

"Just … playing around."

"Show me!" Hy glimlag, stel belang. Hoekom, wonder sy. Sy maak die skerm wakker en wys hom die eerste raam.

"Nothing out of the ordinary," merk hy op. Sy oë soek hare, 'n frons tussen sy wenkbroue.

"What are you playing at?"

Sy kyk moedswillig voor haar uit, antwoord nie. Verklap niks. Mel sug.

"Karin, there's never going to be a day that I'm not intrigued by what is going on in that stubborn head of yours. Tell me! What are you looking for?"

"Nothing, Mel! I'm not looking *for* anything! I'm looking *at* something." Sy swaai terug na die skerm, wys na die deursnit van die spatsel alge.

"Watch this guy," sê sy en gaan terug na die eerste raam. Sy klik deur die eerste ses, dan stadiger. Agt, nege, tien.

"Why did you go back?" vra Mel, sy oë op die skerm gefokus.

"I didn't, Mel. Watch." Sy gaan voort, raam elf, twaalf, dertien. Die blom-alge krimp al hoe kleiner en kom tot stilstand by vyftien. Dan begin dit weer swel, sestien, sewentien, agtien. By negentien blom dit oop. Dan, op twintig, krimp dit weer terug.

"Am I imagining this? Is it possible?" Sy kyk om, vas in Mel se peinsende oë.

"It's beating, Mel."

"That's impossible, Karin!"

Sy voel die hulpeloosheid opbou—dinge wat sy sien en nie kan beskryf nie, dinge wat sy weet en nie kan verdryf nie. Skielik, die stem van binne:

Verval. Verweer.
Begin. Oorgee.
Begin weer. Al is dit seer.
Alleen wees is 'n leuen.

***

30 Junie — "Galley"
Karin en Thlologelo is op skottelgoeddiens. Hulle saamwees is geolie. Hulle hoef skaars te praat. Tussen aangee en was, afspoel en wegpak, is daar oomblikke vol vrae wat net die lyf kan vra. 'n Huiwering wanneer hulle hande raak. Asem wat ingetrek word wanneer hulle oogkontak maak. Uiteindelik, versigtig: klein dapper woorde.

"T, I've been hearing voices. One voice, actually. More specifically. I ..."

Die stil oomblik van iemand wat liefhet, wat verwarde gedagtes kans gee om te bedaar. Uiteindelik 'n vraag:

"Yes, K-bear? You ... what?" Trane. Verligting, vrees, verlange.

"I didn't want to wake up, T! I didn't fall by accident, I ... jumped." Sy pers die woord uit haar keel net voor die snikke oorneem. Thlologelo se seephande hou haar vas, haar skouer bied 'n toevlug. Etlike minute staan hulle so ineen gevleg voordat die vraag die oomblik kan ontmoet.

"Did the voice tell you to jump?" vra Thlologelo saggies. Karin lig haar kop, vee haar neus af met haar mou. Lag.

"No, T. It called me back."

"It wasn't attacking you?"

"No, it's been a guide, really. It ... gives words to things I don't know how to explain. It only started speaking to me when I was under the water, when I thought it was ... done. And since then, it keeps coming back, keeps adding more words."

"Really? What does it say?" Karin se gesig rus in Thlologelo se hande.

"It ... speaks about growing and giving. How being alone is a lie." Thlologelo byt saggies aan die binnekant van haar wang, voel haar pad na die grense van alleenwees se bang. Glimlag, want die waarheid maak nie net vry nie. Dit maak heel.

"Join me outside, won't you?"

30 Junie — Dek

Dis 'n stil aand. Die sterre strek wyer as die horison en Karin voel hoe haar bors swel van die koue. Die skip is op die oop water en die sterlig verdubbel verby die handreling. Sy draai haar gesig na die donker en kyk hoe haar asem dans in die maanlig. Haar trane vries op haar gesig. Die geruis van die wind weef deur die geraas in haar kop. Die ritmiese klap van die enjin spoeg rook die nag in. Sy ruik dit, al kan sy dit nie sien nie. Sy onthou haar val deur die sterre. Haar wakker word, sonder keuse. Die enjin word stil, en skielik is daar ruimte om haar. Tyd om te kyk hoe 'n blaar oopvou, hoe 'n blom en 'n by mekaar onthou. Die aarde dans tog om die son op 'n ritme wat vir biljoene jare al vasstaan en hou. Sy kyk na Thlologelo langs haar, voel haar hand binne haar eie. Sy lag. Amper waansinnig, só vol van blydskap. Niemand hoef dit te glo behalwe sy nie. Sý weet dat sy weet, al maak dit hoe seer: sy *lewe.*

Weer (en weer) verweer.
Weer verweef, verteer
en verskeur,
meer verweer.

Kom terug.
Kom weer.
Jy groei.
Ek gee.

Verval. Verweer.
Begin. Oorgee.

Begin weer, al is dit seer.
Alleen wees is 'n leuen.
Weer verweer, saam verweef.

Stadiger leef.

Begin oor. Leef weer.

4

Boreas Box-17

Yuwinn Kraukamp

Her anxious emerald eyes stared through the snow-speckled porthole to her left, and leered at the white, wintery hell on the other side of the glass. The Antarctic landscape seemed more alive and incensed today, as if the frozen wilderness out there knew something September didn't. But should have.

"I came on this research expedition for the same reasons as all of you," she said to the men and women staring up at her. To the group of glaciologists, marine biologists and climatology students that breathed in her every word. "For the same dream."

Commanding and supervising a group of individuals from different nations and different fields, was unfamiliar territory to September. Her element was the lab-ice-breaking cleaver in hand, algae beneath her microscope, and a Frank Ocean playlist in her ears.

"Twelve months ago, we launched twenty Boreas boxes into the marginal ice zone all around us. And these data-capturing boxes, thanks to our mechanics from UCT, have been doing deep-sea scans and observations of the atmospheric effects that the sea-ice pancakes in this zone have had on the ocean's chemistry. And the good news is that it worked," September proudly announced to scattered applause.

"Seventeen has been relaying very, very promising data. And that valuable, atmospheric data will allow us to build more accurate climate-change algorithms, capable of predicting snowstorms, heatwaves and other environmental catastrophes months in advance," she said with unmistakable hopefulness. "So, everything we've been working towards for months, everything we need to save as much of this world as we can … is in box seventeen."

The beautiful brunette's voice deepened when she revealed the real reason she had summoned them all into this briefing room: "The bad news, however, is that box seventeen is not retrievable at the moment. As you all know, we have a sea-diving drone that's designed to go down there and collect the Boreas boxes, but for the last few days, we haven't been able to pick up box seventeen's locator beacon, and the drone needs that signal to find number seventeen."

The group immediately became rattled and panicked as desperation and doubt filtered through the room.

"The box's navigation system malfunctioned, but we all knew this mechanical difficulty could happen under these conditions," September continued to explain. "So, we're gonna have to manually reactivate the locator for the drone to retrieve box seventeen."

"Manually?" asked an agitated engineer. "You mean, someone will have to reactivate the beacon by hand? One of us, I'm guessing?"

"Yes," September sombrely replied.

"That's suicide! Even if we had the diving gear, or the training—which we don't—diving into that ice-cold water is suicide." The smart-ass naysayer wasn't saying anything September hadn't already considered.

And then came the million dollar question: "So who's crazy enough to do that?"

An unsettling silence swept through the room like a bad odour.

"As the leader of this expedition, all its problems are my responsibility, so … I'll do it," she said as persuasively as she could.

In that moment September chose bravery, and obligation over terror. In that moment she felt like the uncompromising eco-warrior she had come out here, to the icy edge of the Earth, to be. And boy did that moment feel good, until her eyes were drawn towards that snow-speckled porthole once again. Towards the icy hell, waiting on the other side.

No one in the room agreed with September's risky plan, especially Kasparow Cupido. He wore his dissent like a dark, heavy crown above his crow-black hair—a facial warning sign for anyone who dared to spark up a conversation with this broody-looking bastard. Unlike everyone else in that room, Kasparow doubted her plan for two very valid reasons: firstly, he was the on-board safety officer of this expedition. Secondly, and more complicatedly, he was September's ex.

Kasparow waited at the back of the briefing room for the beanie-clad group of scientists to return to their stations, and once the last boot had cleared the room, he slowly approached September.

"Are you insane?" he asked under his breath. "You know damn well those diving suits weren't designed for those depths." His voice rose with fierceness, "The water pressure alone will rip your suit apart." And rose again, ultimately breaking: "And then the freezing temperatures down there will crush every nerve in that body of yours." After all these years, after their pain and plummeted vows, Kasparow still cared for her. "September, you could—"

"—I know," she whispered. "I know what could happen."

Kasparow's confoundedness bled into rage: "Then WHY—THE HELL—are you doing it?"

"Because someone has to," she said determinedly. "Because it's the right thing to do," she said, knowing full well that she was speaking to the angry, hopeless part of Kasparow that never understood why she would risk her life for any theoretical hope.

"There's a reason we send a drone, a machine, into that seawater and not people. People can't survive down there. You're not a bloody white walker, September. PLEASE ... just ... just ask the mechanic to do some McGyvering and fix the damn drone!"

"The drone isn't broken, Kaspar," she gently corrected him. "It can only find box seventeen if the locator beacon is active. Without that beacon, the drone's navigational system will be useless—entirely blind beneath all those ice pancakes. A machine won't save us this time."

"You're throwing your life away. And for what? For who?"

"For the world! The data gathered in that box down there could help us create more precise weather-predicting modules, which would help us remedy so much of this climate crisis. Think about the droughts, and the storms, and the agricultural horrors that we'd be able to prevent with a module like that. Think about the thousands of people back home that we'd be able to help." She tempted his dark soul with her undying hopefulness. "But it all starts with the sea-ice data in that box. Box seventeen is how we begin to save the world."

"Maybe the world doesn't want to be saved," he whispered, dejection vibrating through his voice and glimmering behind his ink-black eyes. "I mean, look around you! The planet is burning as we speak, and the majority of humanity doesn't give a single shit! They're too busy posting TikTok videos, exploiting each other, and plainly killing one another, even as we stare down the barrel of the gun. So maybe ... maybe the world doesn't deserve to be saved. Maybe we never did."

Her heart shattered for him. "You don't believe that, Kaspar. You can't."

"No," he shook his head. "No. You don't get to tell me what I can and can't believe anymore. Those days, of you making assumptions about what's inside my soul ... about whether I have one at all, are over."

"I know you lost your faith in this world, but I also know there's a part of you that still cares, Kasparow. The part that still believes in people—in this world. I've seen it." She reached forward and pressed her fingertips against his chest. "I've touched it. You became a safety officer for a reason. Keeping people safe is what you do, Kaspar. You're a saviour, like me."

"No, I'm not," he grimly disagreed. "My job requires me to envision the hundreds of ways that do-gooders like you can get themselves killed in rainforests, and deserts, and frozen wildernesses like the one out there! When you look at Antarctica, you might see some beautiful ecosystem to study, but my job is to prepare for the worst-case scenarios. For the infections and the viruses. The food shortages and the engine failures that lead to a sinking ship. I have to see all the disasters; all the ways Antarctica can kill you. And make no mistake, September, everything out there wants to fucking kill you!"

"If you truly believe that, then why come along?"

"Because I'm getting a proper pay-cheque. And because ... you asked."

"Right," she murmured. "Isn't risking one life, to spare generations, a worthy risk?" She paused for an answer she wouldn't get, then, "I'm diving at dawn."

***

Each time September closed her eyes that night, she was startled awake by the suffocating feeling of water entering her lungs. That her bed had turned into an iron sarcophagus, sinking to the bottom of the sea. She splashed her weary face with water and stared at herself in the bathroom mirror with eyes that could burn holes through her own reflection.

"You can do this," she quietly encouraged herself. "These are just nerves ... that's all. There's a reason you were chosen to lead," she reminded herself aloud.

September gulped down cup after cup of coffee until her alarm clock went off, and the moment of truth arrived. She marched through the grey hallways with her most convincing game face, masking her frightened features. September hardened herself with every step to keep her fear from ripping her innards apart. She reached the equipment room, and the moment she stepped inside she immediately sensed that something was very wrong. The shelf where the bright-orange diving suits were hung was disheveled. And when she took a closer look, she noticed that of the four suits, one was missing.

She rushed to the exit leading to the ship's deck, and the instant she looked through the porthole at the top of the metal door, all her fears were confirmed: she saw a large man, fully clothed in a diving suit, standing on the deck. She couldn't see his face, but knew with agonising clarity it was Kasparow.

Like a woman possessed, September banged her fists on the steel door he had locked from the outside. "KASPAR! KASPAROW!" She screamed. "LOOK AT ME!"

Kasparow turned his head and looked at her, briefly, before turning away again and walking towards the edge of the icebreaker. Kasparow had hoped to be in the water before September got to the equipment room, before she had a chance to try and stop him, making this harder than it already was. Unfortunately for him, September was a stubborn and determined woman. Remembering that the suits have an internal communications network, she ran back to the equipment room.

She grabbed the helmet of the first suit and brought the microphone to her mouth. When September switched on the comms system, she immediately heard Kasparow's heavy breathing through the earpiece.

"Kaspar," she called out to him. "What are you doing?"

In truth, September knew exactly what he was attempting: he was trying to protect her by taking her place.

"What the hell are you doing?" she asked desperately.

"I'm gonna reactivate the locator beacon," he said through his own microphone. "I'm gonna try to be a saviour. Like you said."

"But you're not a saviour. That's what you said."

"No, I'm not. But I think you are."

"I don't need you to save me, Kaspar. I'm not some damsel in distress. I'm the leader of this group, and I'm perfectly capable of reactivating that signal an—"

"—I know you can. But going into this water was always gonna be life or death," he said as he stared down at the deep, black waters before him. "Not every life is equally valuable. Mine, for example, isn't. But yours, September ... the world can't afford to lose your intellect, your research and your annoying ability to always do the right thing. It can't afford to lose your heart."

"You're breaking mine right now, Kaspar," she tearfully confessed.

"I know," he breathed out. "I'm sorry."

Kasparow placed his boot on the railing, and prepared to dive in. But before he did, he needed to say goodbye in his own way. "You should know that um ... that I loved you," he said, raw with regret. So many regrets.

"If you love me, why do this?"

Kasparow hoisted himself onto the railing, suspending his whole body right on the very edge.

"Because it was never enough," he answered her, and dived in.

September ran back to the porthole, just in time to see Kasparow's body disappear beneath the icy surface. She watched the sea swallow his entire figure in an instant, as if he had never been there. Through that ice-coated glass she watched, feared and wondered if the sea would ever give him back to her.

5

Mimi, Captain's Log

Mehita Iqani

November 20, 2047, 57°S 14°E
Here there is no stillness. There is only motion. Change is our constant.

The steel cloud presses into heaving, abstract clashes of saltwater whipped by screaming wind.

And through this dense meaning of cold, the shape, sound and texture of minus degrees: an icebreaker. *My* icebreaker. Mimi and her crew, on a mission to liberate some packs and pancakes.

In this heated world, what commodity is more precious than ice?

November 21, 2047, 59°S 23°E
The Ice-Cold War started when the Antarctic Treaty was broken. Five years ago, today. We each toasted a whiskey-finger in the galley, to mark the grim anniversary.

2042: nuclear warships from three belligerent nations crossed the 60th parallel south. It started as a show of adventurous military might. "Our RIGHT to Explore!" was the cocky catchphrase, but soon enough the real motives shone through. Ice prices were surging. With none left at the north pole, all the extractocrats looked beadily south. The nouveau-populists, those fascist fuckbois who rigged and jigged systems to take over erstwhile democracies, wanted a new slice of the south polar pie to stick a flag in. First, they jostled, then they scratched each other's backs and drew up new imaginary lines across the White Continent and the Southern Ocean, keeping the conflict on ice if everyone stuck to their own shelf.

Five years later, the war has crystallised into this rigid pattern: the subs and warships flex at each other from a distance, patrol and harvest their parcels, and collaterally damage whatever creature is in their way. Their fire power is rarely discharged, but always in view. While they war over the right to chisel the fast ice and scoop the floes, our nimble, clever boat dodges, nets, retreats, quietly picking up crumbs from the edges.

With sailorly savvy and the ageing but solid tech on our trusty, sharp-bowed ship, our blue-green-grey razzle-dazzle, we've dodged the subs' crosshairs. So far.

November 22, 2047, 60°S 31°E
Ice-mining is illegal.

That is, if anyone but the masters of the nuclear subs does it.

They call it the 'International Ice Extraction Partnership' but if you ask us, IIEP is just another front for claiming the commons.

According to this "law"—as unjust as any other robber baron diktat—we're "stealing" ice because only licensed "partners" can "harvest". The real muggers are those brutes with gaudy epaulettes stuck to their Gore-Tex shells, carrying AKs and RPGs, stomping snow off their golden pumpkin boots, kicking penguins, brazenly overseeing the forced calving of tonnes of ice and its loading onto the megabreakers, which then heave mercilessly back through the shuga, towards home country ice markets. There, prices are set centrally, and supply is controlled at ice-ration stations.

Mimi and her crew? We're free to steal and trade. We were lucky to have been out on the open ocean when everything changed. The scientists overwintering when the treaty was shattered are now indentured with unforgiving martial commanders, their expertise forcibly extracted, their labour captive to this military-industrial freeze economy. As soon as we learned about the ice-rush, we went sub-comms to reorganise our lines of command. We debated for days until we agreed on our modus. They voted me Captain. My fourth re-election now. I've told everyone I'm retiring once this year is up.

High winds bawl, heavy waves batter this line that touches no land. They offer cover for our stealth.

I hold Mimi on the 60th for now. We'll ride this side, following the silver twilight east into the horizon, letting the wild westerly backwind our engines. Though fuel is low I can stretch what remains to last this mission.

November 23, 2047, 60°S 42°E
Beyond: ice disks float in startled geometry, trading shades of pale blue. Beckoning.

My pretty ship, my brave little icebreaker, safe in her clever dazzle dress. Gently nudging these floes until it's time to start netting.

The polar nights are long enough and the swell high enough to hide behind. We've been tracking the subs, mining-ships and megabreakers. I'm confident that we're in unpatrolled sea ice. Mimi's been dark since sunset. When the ice fog arrives deep past midnight, we will unwind the winch and drop the nets. On average we catch two dozen pancakes a shift. Tonight, we'll aim for three. The team is silent, practised. Everyone knows their role, their place.

We're ready. In two hours, we go.

November 24, 2047, 58°S 39°E
The damned nuke-sub surprised us as we were hauling out the last batch of pancakes. We gave as good a shock, I know. They must've just been coming up for a moonrise—no way could they have read past our sonic-shield. It was a strange stand-off. Mimi's whole crew froze in the act.

The sub opened comms on its loudspeaker with an aggressive missive to identify. Torpedo turrets swivelled our way.

I loudspeakered back that we were allied indentured scientists. I announced their confidential vessel code, which my crack team had hacked and read into my earpiece, signalling that because we knew their identity, location and reporting structure ahead of time, we outranked them. Working undercover, I said, top secret mission, need-to-know basis. They could check back with HQ to confirm.

The gun sights blinked. I told them we'd be done shortly, and that there would be hell to pay from the Commander for whoever delayed us. That he'd strip the brass of any low-ranking subsailor captain who'd squealed.

They floated firm, watching. We finished netting fast.

I gave the signal to raise the nets, and within three minutes the winch and team were back on board. We saluted the sub, then powered unhurriedly but fast as we could north-east. When we were out of sight into the slush, we zigged directly north-west, sending off a decoy signal in the other direction.

By the time they confirmed (if they were savvy enough to try) we were not what I'd said we were, we'd be long gone.

It was too close a call.

I'll call a special meeting. The crew needs new leadership.

And yet: three hundred kilograms of ice in the store. A decent bounty to end my tenure.

December 10, 2047, 40°S 23°E
We live off this white market trade, up-ocean well north of the 50s, where the hot and sweaty brokers meet us in warmer waters on their shiny superyachts, ready to pay top dollar for our polar bounty. Sales are swift. We slice and saw chunks in the freezer, weigh, cost and take air-cash, then transfer the goods in insulated boxes marked "FINEST SOUTHERN SNOEK". They sail home, ready to re-sell at eyewatering markups.

Our takings are evenly split. Each crew member converts, encrypts and banks their share. I'll do the same, then pack my gear and say my goodbyes. My brother will meet me in international waters two days sail west of here, with my beloved 30-foot *Cami*.

Then, we'll meander back to my mooring in the plastic barrel jetty that's replaced the sunken harbour, and I'll settle in to rub off the salt and reacquaint myself with the heat simmering off the flat-top mountain.

Mimi and her new Captain (Crystal: excellent choice) and old crew will head back towards the Antarctic circle to liberate a new load from the Ice-Cold War. Perhaps someday I'll come back out to see them in the guise of a buyer. That's if the well-heeled yachties leave any ice slabs for the likes of me.

6

The Reigning Ice

Linda Lee Mhlongo

I sat, forlorn, on the unsympathetic ice shelf, thinking of how events had unfolded in the last few days. The bright light reflecting on that vast expanse of ice shone for hours, making it hard for me to tell the time. There was no night. My teeth and knees were composing a song too deafening to hear, with dismay written all over the melody of fear. I could do nothing but wonder if anyone would find me, rescuing me from a nightmare that knew no limits. In that part of the world, the winds are violent and unbearable, and for a tiny person like me, with nothing to hold on to, staying stable on that ice sheet was a mission reserved for those who have dared to reach the apex of Kilimanjaro. But I was at the core of the Antarctic.

I was shattered. I couldn't think straight. All my colleagues lay buried under the ice. With no one to comfort me, I stood shivering. That sturdy ship, trusted with its stability and technology, enabling my team and I to collect and catalogue our data, had sunken deep into the belly of the cold and calculating waters of the Southern Ocean. We had underestimated that part of the ice. And I would not allow their loss to have been in vain. For that data, I had to survive against odds, I thought, as I looked at the sun that seemed to be fading slowly, which meant the past five days were the last of summer, and winter was approaching. Far away, the science community waited with bated breath for an outcome that could advance its efforts to untangle the consequences of global warming.

"The ice will be gone by 2042," I remember warning. "We must make haste and conclude all the tests and prepare for the rest."

That was before we set sail, enthusiastic and armed with the state-of-the-art equipment we had invested our scientific ideas in. We'd been there before. The expeditions had been successful, and the predictions had been close to accuracy. But there I was, alone. With only my thoughts keeping me company. I thought of home, the world I was likely to never return to, my children, and the colleagues I'd never see again and the projects we'd never realise.

I wondered how these dynamics could have failed with the optimisation of a cutting-edge icebreaker. The combined dynamics of bioprocessing, oceanography and precision engineering were carefully merged as disciplines that could help man man-up against the self-inflicted degradation of the planet. "But it's a marginal ice zone, and the margins run thinner against the sinner. Miracles must come to existence before persistence runs to negligence. Right, Oratile?" Those were Josh's last words. It was the second-last day of the expedition. How could such a good day have turned so bad?

I looked yonder, staring at nothing, thinking that there had to be something to carry me away. Otherwise, who would tell of the crew's heroism before tragedy struck? Two days had passed, and how I was still alive was anyone's guess. No water, no food, no sound, except for the howling wind and the intrusive voices in my head.

The echo of the screams as the ship went down still raises the hairs on the back of my neck.

Something violent had happened, something we had not been expecting. It started with the ship gaining speed, an unusual speed, pushing against the thick ice, and breaking it like it was mere glass. While we were trying to adjust to that phenomenon and frantically investigating it, the ship took a quick turn that hurled everybody sideways, up, then down. We were still startled and trying to launch the emergency protocol when suddenly the ship began to dive. Only one person was regurgitated by the steel ship's maw during that commotion. And there I was still stranded. The thick ice sheet drifted with me, far away from the site of the disaster. My feet were getting colder, and colder still were the winds in these parts that knew no man.

There had to be an escape somewhere. I didn't think that I'd been spared only to die a lonely, slow and agonising death. The ice sheet seemed to be floating towards land. That gave me hope. As if I was on a calm river, the ice raft gently butted into the shoreline, coming to a halt, allowing me to jump off onto the next stop—land ... or the next best thing in Antarctica, fast ice. Feeling somewhat safe, I began to feel the hunger pangs, and the unbearable dryness of my mouth.

Determined to survive, I thought I should explore my surrounds. Perhaps I could find something, anything, that could help me. So, despite the piercing pain in my legs, I dragged one foot in front of me, and then the other, and then the other. It was important that I kept moving if I was to survive. Someone had to tell the story, even if it was unpalatable, I told myself. "I am a woman, *imbokodo*, and I shall not stop until I drop," I willed myself to hope.

Even the wind began to understand the reasons forbidden by the nameless and faceless creature that pulled the ship down. It had to be a creature, otherwise what else could have sunk the gigantic ship so fiercely in the Antarctic where everything floats? Consolidated ice could attest to that without shame. Forward I went, carried by a gentle push of the wind that had become friendly, at least at that moment. I was still struggling to drag one foot at a time when I began to slide. I opened out my arms to regain balance, as the speedy yet gentle wind continued to propel me forward towards new horizons. For a while I forgot about the mechanics of nature and scientific principles and enjoyed the unusual and pleasant phenomenon that swept me across the surface with ease.

I was still enjoying the ride when my sudden skating stunt began to turn into yet another nightmare. The wind that had been propelling me forward was no longer gentle, instead it started to push me around erratically, causing me to lose balance. I wanted to scream but no sound came out of me. Off I skidded, and then fell, hitting the frigid floor hard. Out of the clatter of clumsiness came darkness, numbness and then silence. Everything went dead quiet.

I must have been out for hours when I was awakened by the cold, and a vice grip on my leg. Something was pulling me. My eyelids were heavy with ice that had settled on my lashes. I couldn't see. I heard the snarl though. It was the whiskey noise that woke me up. Realising my imminent demise, I started to scream at the top of my lungs. Except no sound came out of me. It must be the creature, I thought, the hope in me dying. The creature was dragging me by the leg, and I could feel my head banging on bumpy terrain, my arms feebly outstretched against the pull. Then the thing began pulling me by both legs, and I could feel its heavy stomping on the thick sea ice. Its snarl becoming louder.

"Stop!" I screamed. My voice having chosen a convenient time to return. "What about the treaty? What about the treaty?"

But on the dumb creature dragged me, farther and farther away from the wreckage. "The Antarctic Treaty ..." I muttered, helpless and hopeless. The sun and its beauty were a thing of the past now. It was dark, and all I could make out of my surroundings were silhouettes.

I thought about the pancakes that lay scattered afar, "If only I could free myself and cling to a nearby pancake," I wondered. Surely the brine would help steer me away from this creature. I was contemplating that escape plan when I heard human voices.

"Which way should we do this? Are we going to use the process lab or the simulation lab?"

"What?" I said faintly, frantically searching for the speakers.

"Agulhas II is tired of our night celebrations, we should consider using our German partners' vessel."

But there was no one but me and the creature dragging me to the unknown. These had just been voices in my head.

7

Two Poems

Boitumelo Riet

SA Agulhas' Girl

I burn all my boats chasing after you
Mama's fear—the vast mouth I sail to
Papa's apprehensive joy
Mane's wall cracking lamentations

the way leads to the Antarctic,
I must remind them
not the whirlpools of my ancestors'
sorrows still scourging

you changed owner and surname,
from Agulhas to the lady who breathes
song for Africa

I too have been repossessed,
re-figured to smooth through
turbulence and cut imperfection

your horn rattles me
from a stupor of slaving
yesteryears

Fiery ferry,
what makes you think I'd miss your
red coloured hulls?

my curiosity cures me of
their restlessness,
about you

Mama cut the cord at the shores
leaving behind my bearings and bonds
Papa laughs like a mad scientist
to have been elemental in my making

Agulhas, your moorings enrapture me now
the harbour is not where I halt but where
our tides begin

the ice awaits me to core at its soul

I leap toward the nightmarish stories
of caressing a frozen deck with both my hands

I am salvaging all of the girl saving herself
from her uterus freezing,
growing an icy heart
& frostbite

all because I am
dreaming of a nourished tomorrow

Unfreeze my Heart, Icebreaker: A contrapuntal

Let me sing your song

to the barren field
of where I'm from

to the hollow
where my starry night schemes
do not yield green
or dancing figurines,

Injected with warm nectar
Cascading streams

of cow's milk and honey bees

Let me cry your tomorrow song

at the unploughed furrows
of my big black block

where shacks are packed
& children no longer swing

or disappear with marbles in their eyes

where fetching firewood is a trap
hatched with empty pockets

and a five bob

Let me sail away to a melody

with my heart frozen
hoisting the cold flag
of your pipe dreams,

Let my ultra voice pierce
and seep into the cracks

of all your tired streaks

Let me reach beyond
to undo the ground begetting
this dead root

Half-winged and aching,
Let me carry you in tunes
& shoulder the shrills you echo

I become restless
when the course is uncharged

So, let our polar travels trail a composition
that writhes a dream open with fresh brine
& watch the beautiful ones feast again

Let these starved dreams make their way
to the belly of my filling song

hear them rumble
hear their waves spiral
yearning to scrape for marvel

A dream that black
does not catch

the matchlight of a township's eyes

Yet wanes the youthful heart.

Let me hail the promising sound
of your horn

To the waters where
heart slates are shaped

With the sharp cut of your blade

Let us plunge into the sounds
of the singing bird, where

the wondering skies that
submerge with the waiting gravel

Untethered with fear

On board, to unshaming horizons

& slice feverishly into frozen dreams

Brine

Campbell Meas

The heat creeps, finger by finger—clawing across the treacle rug—
her ankle exposed, a slow and steady pulse clear—a homing beacon.
The creaking wood had felt glacial underfoot when she first stepped
into the room carrying a squirming bundle that cooed against the
sleep her mother was trying to rock her into. On the rug she had
found respite for her stockinged feet, having left the dusty heels at
the door, she didn't want to walk death into the room with her. It
had followed all week and here in his office, where his proud ... tired
body had been found slumped in the armchair, she could instead sit
with her regrets and converse with his.

Heavy darkness is what she wrapped herself in, the crackling of
tinder and crumbling coal starting a tune she couldn't follow along
to—her eyes straining to read her own handwriting—*what was I
saying here?* Maybe three or four lines back—there she would find
the trail, something to grasp onto and this time she'd promise to
follow the thread. She searched her own words for a way to fill
the gap—a quarrel that had grown into a rift that reconciliation
couldn't find six feet under.

The light the infant fire promised eventually arrived; the
darkness envious at how she seemed to shift in her seat with relief.
Her stillness had not been a sign she was content in the dark but
rather betrayed her fear to tread in it.

Here on the floor she—a glacier crumbling under the weight of her own sadness, struggled to move further away from the heat she was tentatively waiting to feel—to put even more distance between herself and the things he last touched. You would think—I mean you would think returning this time would be easier; that the separation, the choppy videos, the missed calls and the texts unsent—not because of unsure fingers but rather bad signal—would all compress into a bursting that they both would give in to. He would fall into the familiar step of guilt tripping, and she wouldn't reach out for a helping hand when scraping her knees—*what was I saying here dammit?*

But not this time. This time, the separation had only cemented the chill in the air that had been growing all these months. The budding heat unwavering in its mission clasped at her ankle. It came unexpected; she had been sitting there longer than she realised. But to move, now? Impossible. Close to calling out for a hand to help her up, she stilled that voice. The voice he had taught her to use unashamedly—getting her practice in, slicing barbs at him from a young age; he would laugh at her cheek, until she began drawing blood. That voice was last heard spewing out of her gut when Matthew had stood and without a skip in his tune casually credited himself for work she had spent hours away from her family hypothesising and confirming. She had just got the news, Matthew not getting out of the way in time, she loosed the acidic sadness on him until he, red-faced, blue-veined and defeated, retreated into the bottom cabins and she staring at the glare of the cold recognised its violence.

She could hear the other voices in the other rooms—the other conversations she would miss and have to smile meekly through the next time they were brought up as a secret handshake between their speakers. She hated those conversations the most. Having to pretend that it was easy sitting, fiddling with her earring, through rehashings of commiserations already spoken. What new thing could truly be gleaned from words already partnered together, forced to link arms in an attempt to relay a fumbling point to begin with? This thought, like the Antarctic wind shearing across her face—became necessary to understand where she was in the scheme of things. Without the wind how could she know they had reached the right pole—the peace of the Arctic frightened her. Here in his room her thoughts knocked against the walls holding the amber shadows of a fire growing confident that the slack remains of a previous day could sustain it.

The beating of the pulse in her ankle quickened—the only signal she trusted when she was back home. Her daughter stirred in the bassinet near the family photos he had put up so proudly—her daughter would awake every afternoon to aunts and uncles looking past her to the minibar that emptied quicker and with growing desperation. Elders frozen in poses that belied their own past carelessness were watching the single set of hands that grabbed, staggered, quietly slipped out bottle after bottle ... they were watching those hands. Those same hands that never picked up her daughter as quickly as those hands used to. And so, this time as her daughter awoke and once again saw the now fire agitated faces of aunts and uncles hovering on the wall above, the baby in the bassinet didn't cry, the crying never made the hands come faster. Ignoring the soldering warmth that was now leaning into her, her ankle began to throb at the heat that was only interested in ensuring she stayed awake. The bottle that glowed green was only interested in putting her to sleep—her daughter sat up right in her bassinet—she was only interested in following along to the song the fire now sang.

Her stomach cramped. A good sign? The voices were dying down their polite sobriety that was a necessary performance when mourning—now they picked up in revelry and joyous cracking of memories of the dead one. They could be heard drilling down, doing their best to get the core of the story that would bring as much laughter and patting on the back as was needed for comfort—*no no: he was an academic at heart, his wife just happened to have a lot of friends—yes yes: she was always his favourite but why with a mouth like that, couldn't they have taught her better manners—maybe maybe: if he hadn't smoked as much we'd be celebrating baby's second birthday instead—poor baby, stuck with a mother like that*—the voices were incessant and so she knew she wasn't leaving this room any time soon. She looked over at his regrets, the drafts of the third dissertation he was struggling to focus on. His wedding ring that had rolled into an unswept corner, she had learnt from the best to be alone. The walls shrunk even more as the heat seared closer to her than her alcohol induced state should've allowed.

Eulogy scrawled on the back of some funding proposal she was in the middle of securing, turning over from her undecipherable handwriting, she now saw how to connect the channel of SAPRI funding to community outreach—her students had always been allowed to run with their ideas, who was she to stop them when those very steps they took also illuminated more of her path. *By recycling the cylinders from last year's trip as a way to setup community water tanks, that will allow ...* Sell people small chunks of a dream that later become the steps to your pathway—when did she first have to start thinking this way? Did she think this way because of him? Had it been him that thought and spoke this way—that she started adopting it as a way to pacify the thoughts that *charity is not giving money, it's action.* His words sat awkwardly now in her numb mouth. Their new owner not quite as articulate. The memory of strangers with the same anatomical tongue but disclosing different tunes that signalled their homes were kilometres of steps away, walking tentatively through her childhood home was something to look back at later, as well as her mother's under-the-breath complaints that these grimy strangers were not the friends she happily offered tea or a beer. Her ankle or head pulsating—a warning light to get up off the rug—traverse the creaking wood floor. *Get up off the floor!*

Why was this heat interested in clinging to her, she had waited for it, needed it but now it felt too needy to deal with—it wanted her attention, to see the red dance that now accompanied its tune, a tune carried by a small voice in the bassinet. Eventually someone will fetch that small voice from the bassinet and bring it to join the other now revelrous voices in the other rooms—she'd get up to kiss her daughter's forehead as those other hands dug into the layers and layers of blankets wringing loosely around her daughter's body, chastising her for hiding the baby away from family. Those voices would coo at her—those hands would pass her around, fix the blankets into a tight weave—these hands needed to reply to the text that came barging into the room—

"God gives his toughest battles to He's strongest warriors.
Nka etsa tsohle ka Kreste ya mphang matla ... Bafilipi 4:13."

Her unsure fingers lingered atop the keyboard—she left the message and went searching for the one she had abandoned a response to—

"When are you coming home—"

She thought for a moment—giving the opportunity for something else to show itself as a viable response rather than the one that now sat on her shoulder watching and waiting patiently to be sent. *Ho tla hae*—coming home had always been—well it had been such a sure thing—the long-term methodology of solve insecurity as a fractal of y could be solved by x, coming home. Now though ... When had she become so unsure of herself—unsure that the homing beacon that marked this place as home, was right this time—the people who populated this home were not people this home was familiar with— the people whose voices she could now hear clearly going through his drawers and cupboards in the other rooms were not the people who had asked just days ago—

"U khutla neng, morali?"
When are you coming home, my daughter?

9

Cold, Cold Woman

David Cornwell

My grandmother lived to the age of 101 and she was a smoker, that shows you the power of grudges, my mother always says, she was a cold, cold woman, my mother says, and I try to think of her again now while I lie with my head turned away from the train window, where it's so cold the water leaking into the top of the frame is making an icy rim against the glass, I'm alone in the compartment except for my school trunk and my satchel with all my books and pens and pencils, which makes it colder, of course, being alone, my mother used to travel with me when I was in primary school and it was better when I could sleep in her lap, but now the sky outside the train window seems too full of stars, like I'm really on some boat at the end of the world, like Shackleton, the man Miss Harvey taught us about whose ship sunk 70 degrees south of the equator in blue-black water, the whole world gets its weather from ice that forms in the sea, it's freezing in here, it feels cold enough for Antarctica, all the millions of icy stars, and finally there's my grandmother in my head, sitting in her chair, always wrapped in a blanket no matter the weather, the point of her cigarette flaring in the room she always kept dark, she had two blankets, one blue, one red, and sometimes she'd use them both, sucking at the cigarette like it was the only source of warmth in the world, she was the quietest person I've ever known,

What are you thinking about, I'd ask her, while she just sat in her chair all day in the dark room,

Who says I'm thinking, she'd ask me back, and I suppose that's kind of how I feel right now, it doesn't feel like I'm thinking it's so cold, it's like my thoughts have slowed all the way down, they've frozen up and the pictures inside my head have gone dark, someone pulled the plug on the carousel, I guess, I'm saying words to myself like Bathwater, like Hot Sweet Tea, but it's all wet kindling, nothing is catching, and I know if I move, if I could just sit up and move to get my trunk and open the latches there is another blanket inside there and my school coat with the thick wool, but my feet are dead as ice blocks in my shoes and my fingers burn in the knuckles as I hold myself and shiver, a cold, cold woman,

So how did she get that way, I asked my mother, maybe a year after my grandmother had died, back at home for the school holidays, the last few days, when I'd start to feel twisted in my stomach, sad already about leaving, my grandmother's room empty for the first time, the curtains open, and my mother told me about when my grandmother was a girl, the same town I was born in and my mother was born in but in the past, my mother called it a different time but it sounded like a different world, a far-off place like the South Pole where the rules were strange and cruel, my mother looking so much like my grandmother as she spoke, her whole face pinched around the ember of her cigarette, and she

052

told me that when she was a girl, my grandmother was very naughty,

Like me, I asked, which was really a joke but my mother didn't smile,

Naughtier, she said, and it looked like she didn't want to say any more but it also looked like she did want to tell me, finally, so naughty, actually, that when she was about your age they had to take her to a special hospital,

What kind of—

They don't have them anymore, she said, it was a different time, she said again, and then my mother who never touched me except to brush my hair held my hand as she spoke, she was dressed up like she was going to church, she said, petticoat and a hat, but then as soon as she got to the sanatorium two sisters made her take off all her clothes,

Even her underwear,

Yes, and they took her to a small room where there were no chairs, just two more sisters in their white-white uniforms, and a blanket lying on the floor, folded into a big triangle, and the sisters told her to lie down but she didn't want to, she said she could feel something was wrong, the blanket was all dark and wet,

Why,

They had soaked it in ice,

Wh—

They used to think it was good for you, and then my mother explained how the two sisters took my grandmother's arms and the other sisters came forward and they took her legs and they put her into the blanket, where the cold was an electric current, a blowtorch all over her skin, and the sisters folded her in the blanket, swaddled her like a baby, she said she couldn't breathe because it was like swallowing blades, she felt the blanket sticking to her skin and the whole world was pain, the blood was aching in her veins even as her heart started to beat slower, and slower, my mother said, and then she let go of my hand and she went into the kitchen and lit another cigarette, and I knew we were finished talking about it, and the first thing I did was go back to my grandmother's room, where the curtains were open and she was gone, but I imagined her, somehow seeing her more clearly than ever before, swimming out on her own in the darkest and coldest of seas, her small head bobbing between the giant, jagged sheets, her raw heart, her lungs, I imagined her reaching out and even touching the other shore, and how when she came back, she never warmed up, not really, and how different the world must have seemed to her, and herself, how different, how ugly, when they finally let her out of the blanket, and now the ice from the top of the window has grown down the side of the glass in a skim, a smeary shutter on all the bright stars, and the train compartment feels very dark, and deep, and I finally stop shivering, I'm just numb, silent and numb, a ship sinking down, down under the dark ice.

10

Winter: An Icy Ally

Tshepo Molefe

Beware the cold front.
A feverish fiend,
pushing warm frenemies
in its unyielding stride.
The clouds follow suit
in propelling their pace.

Their objective:
to test the formation of boys
gathering on a mountaintop.
You too will be asked to join
their journey to manhood.

Remember,
some will falsify their bravery.
Will choose to declare themselves
"strong".

They are yet to know
the weather's chisel.
She is far too familiar with
extracting innocence
seeped in their brine.

But you know better.
You know this venture
promises turbulence.
Will stress your character
to the point of breaking.
The nobility in your word
will strain.

Don't be deterred.
Winter was not made
for your unravelling.
It has come to uncover your core.
The harshness will build you up.
The cold will remind you
of your resistance.
Let it build you into ice
that outlives seasons.

Then tell summer
to do its worst.
Now you know
you can stand
the test of
time.

11

The Mushy Layer

Lee Middleton

The mushy layer is where it all happens. And yes, that is the scientific term, despite it sounding like something a five-year-old might say. You know, the mushy layer: The banana destined for the compost. The wall spongy with mould. The wet spot. Life's messy chaos made visible if you can stand to look at it, which, frankly, most of us do not desire. I mean, who has the time between swiping and wiping and blitzing kale smoothies?

Scientists have largely overlooked not only the mushy layer, but the entire strata to which the mushiness is attached; that is, sea ice. The liminal zone separating ocean from atmosphere, sea ice regulates the heat exchange between our planet's largest elements, meaning it's a key part of the machinery stabilising the climate. This is particularly true of Antarctic sea ice, whose formation represents the planet's largest natural event in terms of area. That annual transformation of an expanse of the Southern Ocean twice the size of the continental United States (18–20 million square kilometres) from ice to water and back again plays a supersized role on global weather patterns. Despite all this, climate models still treat Antarctic sea ice as a "black box", which is akin to budgeting for a road trip without knowing the price of fuel.

For insight into this omission, let's start with descriptors like, "the South Pole of Inaccessibility" and "below 40 degrees south there is no law; beyond 50 degrees south, there is no God" (the Antarctic lies below 60 degrees). Encircled by seas infamously roiled by the Antarctic Circumpolar Current (the world's strongest ocean current), Earth's southernmost continent is its coldest (recorded temperatures dive below -80° Celsius) and most remote land mass. Which is to say, this is a place whose truths will not be readily surrendered.

Which makes me think of North Korea. A land that hostile and complex human negotiations have made as unapproachable as geography has rendered the Antarctic. A sense of self-preservation staying any impulse to attempt understanding *that* situation. I mean, who wants to spend even a minute of their wild and precious life bogged down in the whys and wherefores of a country ruled by a triptych of 'Great Leaders' who continue to low-key hold the world hostage with opaque nuclear threats, and are famous for things like banning films from places whose actors were kidnapped to perform for Great Leader #2's personal gratification? Isn't life too short to voluntarily start nosing into questions whose answers—if they even exist—only catapult one into an infinitely blooming multiverse of other questions? It is!

But eventually the cost of ignorance might exceed the seeming impossibility of finding answers. And then what?

***

Nucleation describes the formation of a first crystal, the start of something.

Because nature always seeks to conserve energy and maintain balance, you could say that doing nothing is, by one interpretation, the natural state of things (change is hard!). In the case of sea ice formation, inducing nucleation requires overcoming the ocean's energy stasis: either by dropping the temperature or introducing what chemists call an "imperfection"—something that can break the bonds of status quo, interrupt molecules that were all going about the business of being liquids until that first ice crystal managed to find a foothold from which to chill and invite friends to the huddle.

Foreign particles—a bit of sea junk, an edge of iceberg, an outcrop of land—are imperfections. Agitation—literally shaking things up—is also an imperfection, scientifically speaking.

By that (and other) logic, military occupation must be an imperfection: simultaneously shaking things up and introducing foreign particles. Whatever else you may say about it, war is undeniably the start of something.

The Korean War nucleated from the Cold War imperatives following the Second World War's expulsion of Japanese colonial powers from the Korean peninsula. Its footprint largely mirroring the 10th century boundaries of its ancient predecessor Koryo, Korea in 1945 had the bad luck to still share borders with Russia, China and Japan. In the post-WWII global shakedown, the American-Russian battle to control this strategic territory led to an afternoon in August when two US officers were given a few hours to draw the line that would delineate American from Russian "stewardship" of the Korean peninsula. Supposedly temporary, the 38th parallel North became the gash dividing one people into two nations. Over 70 years later the Koreas are still technically at war. A fracture visible from space, the undisturbed swath of green remains a no-man's land where Amur leopards, Siberian tigers and red-crowned cranes shelter; species too fragile to survive the hungers of our human world.

Crossing no land whatsoever and marking a different kind of no-man's land, the 60th parallel South distinguishes all the inhabited continents from Antarctica below. Defining the northern limit of the Southern Ocean, the latitudes south of the 60th—where winds exceed 145 kilometres an hour and whip up waves towering over five-storeys high—are described as the "Screaming 60s". But even those latitudes are not free from human meddle: the 60th serves as the northern limit of the Antarctic Treaty System, as well as the southern boundary of the South Pacific and Latin American Nuclear-Weapon-Free Zone.

While humanity's treaties and armistices and promissory notes are meaningless to the lifeforms going about the business of survival in the Screaming 60s, the 38th parallel's articulation was the beginning of the end for Korea's inhabitants. The war that followed—killing nearly 10 per cent of the population—is sometimes called the "forgotten war". A moniker that begs the question, forgotten by whom? Certainly not the five to seven million Koreans who survived by scattering to all corners: a handful of jacks tossed across the hot pavement of a bored afternoon. I recently learned that Koreans still top the list of the most internally displaced people—on par with places like Syria and the DRC—a fact that provides context for the expulsion from South Korea of some 200,000 (maybe-probably-mostly-not-really) orphans for adoption to the West, of which I am one.

Growing up in America, I thought I knew what had happened to me, where I came from, who my people were. I was given pictures and names of biological parents who had died from causes—heart attack, cancer—I could grasp. I received letters from older brothers sent to Denmark for adoption; their *par avion* memories captured in a baroque Scandinavian cursive, scraps to quell any adolescent yearning to wonder further about my birth family. But then, later, I did wonder about a few things, and those questions led to the discovery that I was not in fact related to those brothers in Denmark: that their story was not mine, but belonged to some other girl, who remains lost to my brothers-not-brothers. My origins suddenly a black box.

***

So what is it about Antarctic sea ice that is so mysteriously important?

Let's take a step back and recognise that in the rare instance that people think about sea ice, the image most likely to spring to mind is that of a sad polar bear stranded on a shrinking ice floe. But that tragic icon belongs to the Antarctic's doppelganger, the Arctic. While superficially similar, the two are, literally and figuratively, polar opposites. A Jekyll-and-Hyde, Jean-Grey-and-Dark-Phoenix situation. Santa, reindeer and polar bears versus penguins huddling to survive the annual death march.

First, the Arctic is an ocean (not a continent). Second, the Arctic's waters are calm—circumscribed by Europe and North America's northern edges, it lacks the open ocean necessary to generate wave action. These conditions mean Arctic sea ice is thicker, longer lasting and less mobile. Antarctic sea ice by contrast is thinner, far more seasonal, spread out across a vast expanse, and dynamic in its formation. In other words, it's complicated.

Regardless of which pole it calls home, sea ice is frozen saltwater. Although the presence of salt hampers freezing (like a rattling window dooming your descent into slumber, salty ions disrupt water molecules' pull to bond into ice crystals), the Antarctic's winter temperatures (coldest place on earth!) and savage ocean churn provide the perfect conditions for imperfection when it comes to ice-crystal formation. But how the ice crystals agglomerate into millions of kilometres of sea ice is where the mushy layer comes in.

As the top (coldest) layer of ice forms, salt is expelled in brine channels that push ever downwards towards the (warmer) ocean water while the ice thickens up top. This perpetually descending slush—the mushy layer!—is made of ice crystals and brine, with the latter trickling in capillary-like fingers that flow into larger "streamers", which occasionally pool before moving again. A complex and dynamic theatre of heat and energy exchange, the mushy layer plays a vital but still poorly understood role in how ice, seawater and the atmosphere interact. Accurate modelling of the mushy layer is therefore critical to understanding how warming temperatures are likely to affect the formation and melting of Antarctic sea ice, which (largest natural event on the planet!) has a massive influence on the ocean currents, heat distribution and climate patterns that dictate life as we know it.

**

"Ice is quite unforgiving at minus 30," the scientist said, referring to her studies on sea ice mechanics and the conditions that cause its fracture. Such information is vital to the integrity of the icebreaker ships that ferry Antarctic scientists into the Screaming 60s to conduct the research that will—hopefully, eventually—demystify sea ice and mushy layer thermodynamics. With climate-related mega-events coming thick and fast, it may not be enough, but it's a start.

Truth can also be quite unforgiving—at any temperature.

For over a decade I chose to ignore the bleak implications of my brothers-not-brothers story. But then I nucleated, literally. Children being the ultimate imperfection, kicking your ass out of stasis. Eventually I learned that in order to facilitate my departure to America, my documents had been falsified, my family name literally excised from the note my birth family had tucked into the blanket that swaddled me. Rendered *adoptable*, I was put on a plane to the United States. A penguin shipped to the Arctic to be raised among polar bears.

Once considered the "Cadillac of international adoption", Korean adoption practice is now the subject of a Truth and Reconciliation Commission. Investigating the cases of over 350 adoptees who suspect foul play by adoption agencies, the process is happening in tandem with a handful of lawsuits filed by adoptees and one birth mother against adoption agencies and the South Korean state. The charges include negligence, fraud and human rights violations. Sparked by the bad press these cases have stirred, in 2024, the Netherlands closed its doors as a "receiving" country, and China (South Korea's only rival in terms of numbers of children sent for adoption) announced the end of its international adoption programme.

The painful truths animating all of these cases make clear why many prefer to leave the past undisturbed. While my own search has been filled with disappointment and mind-fuckery, it has equally nourished my soul in profound and unexpected ways. It also opened my eyes to a bigger picture in which I understand that we adoptees are the tip of the iceberg when it comes to the forced separations, displacement and intergenerational trauma suffered by Koreans— North and South—over the course of the 20th century. Reading the international news these days, I am frequently struck by how these dynamics continue to play out. Topping the list for the highest suicide and lowest birth rates recorded in the so-called developed word, South Korea—in a panic about its shrinking population—nonetheless continues to send a couple hundred of children for overseas adoption annually. Change is hard.

I take strange comfort in sifting my way through these layers of grim context, which, while failing to yield anything like the specific answers I crave, also belie the power of the black box. That is, by starting to understand pieces of a story whose beginning I may never know, I can perhaps change the ending.

***

Scientists used to think that the mushy layer's brine channels were static, stationary and predictable. More recent studies say not so: the bigger streamers can suddenly shut off. The smaller fingers can change course, moving the brine—with its friction and warmth—to melt an opposite channel; an ever-shifting meander that not only makes sea ice formation possible, but also acts as a nursery where microbial critters and nutrients flourish, stimulating phytoplankton blooms that attract and feed marine creatures from krill to penguins to whales. A whole food web, indifferent to human efforts to understand its inner-workings, thriving in the vast, glorious and ever-mushy crucible of life.

12

FicSci

John Trengove

Outside the glass box of the seminar room the weather turns. The Brilliant Scientist smiles.

"This is my kind of weather. I love the cold."

The day before the forecast had warned of coming storms and as I left the house my husband pretended to be jealous at the thought of me, high and dry in a mountain hotel for the next three days. Hanging out in front of log fires with fellow fiction writers. Having "encounters" with a Brilliant Scientist, learning about science-y things.

"Spare a thought for me and the dog." He kissed me goodbye. "Bored and lonely at home. Missing daddy."

It seemed like a luxurious diversion when I was applying, but as the day drew closer I dreaded the notion of an experimental workshop. What really was the point of a bunch of creative writers learning about sea ice for three days? As always the pressure of work was overwhelming and as usual I was late with almost everything.

In the seminar room, my phone buzzes from a spate of unread emails. Ugh. I switch on Airplane Mode and tune back into the presentation. I'm in this now. Best to keep an open mind. Outside, the wind picks up and the first drops of rain pelt against the insulated windows. My eyes strain in the fluorescent light and I reach for the blanket I'd been handed by the friendly hotel staff. Cosy.

The Black Box. The Brilliant Scientist explains how the atmosphere and the ocean have long been understood and studied as distinct entities. But between ocean and atmosphere there is something much more mysterious known as The Black Box which is, as far as I can tell, the interaction between ocean and atmosphere, in the form of oceanic ice. It has something to do with nucleation vs crystal growth. Shit. The conference organiser, studiously hammering away at her laptop next to me, asks for clarification about nucleation. Relief. Yes, concentrate. You have a moment to catch up here. But the clarification comes and again I miss it. Fuck! What is nucleation? I'm too distracted by the writer sitting next to me. She has some kind of fancy pen, and her handwriting is exquisite. Her notes spread across the page in both vertical and horizontal formations which means she must be extra smart and creative. OK. Focus. The Brilliant Scientist now explains The Moving Boundary Problem. I write down 'Moving Boundary Problem'. This sounds good. Like sea ice, I, too, have moving boundary problems. I can relate. Virality Drainage. Brine pathways through the ice. That's pretty cool. Being the warmer substance, brine melts pathways through the ice and seeps into the ocean. What is brine exactly? Is it salt? Pretty sure I brined a chicken once and it came out delicious.

The Brilliant Scientist flinches. She loses her focus. Did I hear someone say she had a migraine earlier? There's a quiver in her hand as she pauses for a sip of water. What must she be thinking? Explaining her work to a group of writers staring gormlessly back at her. What an odd situation. What are we all doing here? It's a novel concept bringing artists face to face with science to see what happens. Invariably something happens. A reaction. We artists are conditioned to respond creatively to things. We love a disruption. A little multidisciplinary what-what. Even if the outcome is deeply pretentious, we soldier on with our work, forever hopeful that what we do will mean something to someone somewhere. I glance around and see the same existential consternation etched onto the faces of my peers. Well, most of them.

The writer with the fancy pen seems confident, her notes flowing from pen to page in neat, interconnected bubbles. One glance at my own left-handed scrawl confirms that I'm never going to look at these notes again. They are performative. Performing for who though? The Brilliant Scientist no doubt. I'd hate for her to think that I'm not passionate about learning about sea ice. I imagine her and her intrepid huddle of students braving the frozen ravages of the Antarctic, taking and analysing ice samples. She casually mentions discovering a new way of cutting ice while making toast in her kitchen one morning. The filaments inside a toaster heat up to 1000 degrees Celsius and can be used to slice ice one millimetre thick without changing its composition. That's impressive. I write down "toaster".

During dinner the rain pelts down so loud on the roof of the hotel that I can barely hear the polite conversation at my table. I think of my husband and my dog at home, snoring in front of the television —God I wish I was there now. I grab a Merlot from the honesty bar and scribble my name in the book. I consider pausing to make small talk with the novelist and the genre writer around the communal fire but I'm feeling cranky, so I head back to my little room. I turn on the electric blanket. Sleep comes instantly.

A white landscape. An icy sea. I'm on a research ship with the Brilliant Scientist and her intrepid crew. Slabs of ice are hauled into pristine naval labs and cut into millimetre thick slices, projecting and refracting light beams through their delicate crystal formations. The colours are dazzling.

"Daddy."

My dog is at my feet, teetering on the rubber floor, struggling to maintain balance on the undulating ship. Distressed and shivering from the sub-zero temperatures. I can tell from the anguished look on his face that he needs to be taken outside for a poo but we're thousands of kilometres from the nearest patch of grass. Why on earth did I bring him to the Antarctic?

"Daddy. Help. Haruf."

***

Day two of the workshop and the Brilliant Scientist now describes the difficulty of replicating oceanic conditions in a laboratory. Each variable, be it atmospheric, temperature fluxes, water movement, needs to be individually layered into the mathematical model to study the behaviour of sea ice. I take stock of the room. The songwriter and oral poet are both keenly nodding, basking in the thrill of learning new things. Beside me the short story writer's pen has a life of its own, notes flowing deep into the margins of the page. But others have lost some of yesterday's lustre. The playwright stares grimly at his computer screen and next to him the copywriter has nodded off, his head teetering like a bladder on a stick. The Brilliant Scientist notices. She soldiers on with the presentation, but the copywriter's head topples forward and snaps back up with a look of surprise. The Brilliant Scientist takes a sip of water.

"Ice that forms at lower temperatures freezes faster and traps more impurities. Ice that forms at higher temperatures forms slower and has more time to wean out brine and impurities from its structure. This makes higher temperature ice both weaker, and with a higher porosity."

Porosity? What on earth is porosity? I flip back through my notes to see if I missed something. I have a thought to google porosity when I get back to my room, but it's followed by a second thought that I won't. The Brilliant Scientist looks at me and I know she knows this too. We're on opposite sides of an unbreachable divide, she and I. She's in a world of matter and molecules. Wrestling with equations that matter. Matter that matters. She's grappling with the tools of her discipline to discover fragments of truth that point to the construction of an infinite universe and our minuscule place in it. She knows her work is meaningful. The outcome of her research helps determine how weather patterns are predicted which helps farmers which helps all of us. On top of that she's redressing the schism between north and south. The great knowledge gap, entrenched by colonialism, perpetuated by capitalism. It's all so fucking noble. Me, I'm in the world of fiction, hemmed in by the distinct limitations of my own imagination. A decidedly fuzzier universe riddled with anxiety and self-doubt, brought about by the nagging fear that nothing I do really matters. Not really.

The Brilliant Scientist joins our table at dinner that night. She's exhausted from two days of talking but makes a valiant effort to discover more about us. We take turns describing our precarious careers. The Brilliant Scientist smiles and nods. The conversation turns to books we've read and films we've seen. What kind of fiction is she into? She glazes over for a moment and tells us that she hasn't read a novel or watched a film in over three years. Why? Just too busy. Not even television? Not even television, she sighs.

The short story writer checks an alert on her phone. Oh wow. A storm warning. The Stellenbosch valley is flooded, and more than 150 houses are being evacuated. Huh.

I wake up to a deafening drone. The sound is so immersive and shapeless that for a moment I wonder if it is sound at all. Then it registers. It's rain. Gallons of water falling from the sky onto the tin roof of my little room. What the fuck? Outside these four walls is unfathomable chaos. A nightmare of wind and wet and darkness. In here, safety. A small protective box perched on a mountain slope, keeping the horror at bay. The thought is thrilling. Almost arousing. I crank up the electric blanket and drift back under.

"Haruf."

I'm back on the icebreaker, in a small cabin in the bowels of the ship. My dog stares at me from a bunk bed with a fish in his mouth. He spits it out. Chunks of ice fall from the wall. I pick up a piece, but it disintegrates in my hand. Porosity, I think. Huh.

"Time to go home. Haruf."

One look at the dog and a pang of guilt shoots up inside me. I dry my hands on the blanket and give him a scratch behind the ears. His eyes roll back, and he licks the briny crook of my arm.

"Yes. Time to go home," I say. "I'm sorry. I didn't know it would be this cold."

"It's the Antarctic."

"You're right. Guess I should have known."

I draw his little body against mine to keep him warm. A violent thud as the icebreaker collides with something vast and immovable.

The ship's power cuts out and the room capsizes. We tumble into darkness.

***

I'm ice cold. But also, inexplicably, boiling hot. What's going on? I squint through the blackness. The loud droning sound tells me I'm probably back in my room. Yes. It's the rain. Under the covers my flesh is roasted by the electric blanket. Above the covers my arms and face are cold. And wet. I realise that the door to my room has blown open and rain is pouring into the room. Half asleep I stumble from the bed and grab a jersey. I try to close the door, but something draws me outside.

The trees surrounding the hotel flail about in the savage wind. Just ahead, a figure in an anorak and snow boots stands in a clearing among the trees, arms outstretched. How can a person even stand upright under these conditions? I stumble into the rain and before I can focus my eyes, I already know who it is. The Brilliant Scientist is radiant despite the rain pelting her face. Her feet are rooted to the earth and her body shakes, conducting an electric current so powerful that the very trees around her bend from its force.

"Dr Rampai, are you OK?"

The Brilliant Scientist smiles. She seems more than OK. Shivering, squinting through the wetness, I already know the answer to my next question.

"Are you … communing with the storm?"

"It certainly seems like it, sweetheart! Granted, it's all a little silly but you're the one in charge, not me."

"Ugh. I know. I'm sorry. I've always had a problem with endings. Tying things up. Like all that stuff about the dog. Not sure where I was going with that. Not my strong point."

"That's OK. I love the cold."

"Oh right. I remember you said that."

"And also, not everything needs to make sense. We are relentless in our search for unity but sometimes all life is, is fragments. That's something we need to accept about it. And our work."

"That's pretty good! Did you come up with that or did I?"

The Brilliant Scientist winks at me.

"Go back inside, sweetheart. You've done what you can."

Relieved, I turn back to my little bed in my little room. I crank up the electric blanket. Sleep comes quickly.

13

Threshold

Senna-Marie Bosman

*A song in contemplation of the point at which a state of being (or matter)
becomes definitively altered; after what threshold is the writer inspired,
the water made solid, the climax reached, and the boundary breached.*

Is this what it takes to excite?
Is this what it takes to excite
in me

Here there are waves I can't ignore
They agitate and allure
Is this what it takes?

I call for a hand, will you take me
there to where you are?
How to withstand, I am swept off
feet a sudden flare

Oh it's alive
Tell God
the floods arrived
Can we doctor this?
Can we, Doctor?
Can we doctor this?

I reach for calm
This sea objects
This fail gives form
Can we?
Disturb the boundary
Deform the myth
and bend the eyes
to see it with

Is this what it takes
to throw up a storm and spit the salt?
Is this what it takes
to agitate against and to revolt?

It takes an overcoming
Excite with pressure
It takes an overcoming
Dare I ask what it takes to stay?
It takes an overcoming
Excite with pleasure
It takes such overcoming
and what would it take for them to say?
It takes an overcoming
Excite and start again

YouTube

❄

14

Outroduction:
Thinning Ice, Concerning Ice

Mehita Iqani and Wamuwi Mbao

This volume presents the outcome of our third FicSci writing retreat, an ongoing literary science communication experiment that brings art-makers and scientists together for the purpose of enquiry into the physical or environmental laws and processes that structure our world.

As will be evident to any reader who has already engaged with other parts of this volume, our invited scientist, Dr Tokoloho (TK) Rampai, is a specialist in sea ice and has undertaken many expeditions to both the north and south poles—though surely her heart, and indeed the bulk of her precious data, is with Antarctica. Although many forms of discovery hinge on an image of the scientist as explorer, venturing into territories as yet unmapped and little known, there is something about the extreme conditions of this planet's poles that offers an extra touch of the dramatic to the otherwise relatively prosaic notion of the laboratory. FicSci 03 is crammed with insights into what it takes to do science in Antarctica, and what Antarctica means as a whole to our sociality.

Our writers were transfixed by images and narratives of scientific discovery, yes, but also by modern-day tales of adventurous travel into the Southern Ocean, beyond the oceanic boundaries any of us had ever before passed. Along with the journey into the physics, structures, properties and behaviours of sea ice, we also journeyed along with our Scientist on the Agulhas II, the icebreaker that is a scientific and cultural national treasure, property of the people of South Africa, and home to multidisciplinary scientific teams who travel out to Marion Island, the Southern Ocean and Antarctica on annual voyages. All of this was done in the quest to reorient ourselves to the ocean, the creatures that live in and on it, the climate and how it is changing, and more. It is hard to say whether the assembled writers were more stunned by the magnificent icy seascape photos from Dr Rampai's iPhone or the complexity of the equations invented to calculate how sea ice is formed, and melts, and the kinds of conditions under which it breaks. Perhaps it was the combination of both that made the 2024 FicSci workshop the most "intense" one yet, inviting all involved to rethink what we know (and what we don't know) about ice and the polar seascape.

The wild weather imagery that is a character in many of the creations assembled here was inspired not only by the journeying of imaginations into or towards the Antarctic; it was also a product of the howling gales and rain-battered windowpanes at our fingertips. The intensity of trying to wrap humanities' brains and word-orientated modes of communication around the hard properties of the maths and physics that underline crystalline science, was matched only by the intense weather conditions that seemed almost summoned by Muse herself to offer us a smattering of the wild, open ocean in our landlocked retreat. Yes, dear reader, we were ushered in and out of our retreat by gushing rains and howling winds. If you have picked up FicSci 01 (flow) or FicSci 02 (night_sky) you'll recall that this experimental gathering takes place at the back of a pretty little valley just outside Stellenbosch. To get there, one drives up a long, winding and increasingly narrow road to reach Mont Fleur. In the years before, the weather there has been delightful and decidedly un-wintery; in 2024 a massive low-pressure system hit the greater Cape Town area and it rained buckets—no, reservoirs!—by the minute. The unusually inclement weather patterns that marked our stay made us feel truly cut off from the rest of the world.

The collection before you is a product of fierce weather, combined with dreams of high-adrenaline extreme adventuring. It takes narratives of sea-voyaging, mixing them up with challenging and detailed deep slices into the very structure of ice. The result is one we are truly proud of. To be sure, these icy writings muse on multiple aspects of the human condition: the pain of leaving behind, the excitement of seeing ahead, the brace of diving under, the expanse of breathing in, the discomfort of exposure (both physical and emotional), and a broader contemplation of the age of the end of ice. This volume offers a number of new ways of looking at the coldest parts of our world, and bearing witness to how, in this age of climate change, our ice is melting away.

FicSci 03 introduced another new aspect to our experiment. We decided to liaise with a new NRF-funded project, which aims to establish an Antarctic Artist and Writers Programme (AWP) for South Africa. Many other countries that do research on the White Continent have long had such luxuries, but South Africa has not— until now. Hearing of this bold move towards staking a South African writerly and artistic claim to the Antarctic science being advanced collectively by humanity was precisely what inspired us to seek out an Antarctic scientist for FicSci 03. In turn, we have encouraged the writers featured in this volume to apply for the chance of joining that residency. Many more wonderful artistic and creative outputs will surely result from the opportunities being created by the AWP, both for communicating Antarctic science, and for helping to create more possibilities for South African and African publics to get to know, and be inspired by, Antarctica.

Another innovation to FicSci 03 was the invitation of a songwriter. By acknowledging that writing is an expansive practice, that includes multiple forms of creative production alongside those that use words, we were hoping to find new ways to redefine science communication. As you will see from Senna-Marie Bosman's contribution, a song was written at FicSci 03. Its lyrics and musical notation are included for the musically inclined to read it, and play it, but you can also see and hear Senna-Marie performing her composition in a music video funded by the SARChI Science Communication by clicking on the QR code in her chapter.

By this third iteration, as convenors and editors of the emergent work, we feel that the unique contribution of FicSci is becoming perhaps as clear as glaze ice: there is something singularly powerful, fertile and fun that happens when creative writers get a chance to pause with science, to face it, crunch their brain cells to seek routes of understanding into scientific knowledge, and then to be permitted to take that knowledge and build on or transform or create, using their own writerly craft and their own imaginations. It is true that scientists speak a peculiar language, and creatives another, and that translation and interpretation is needed to reach some communion between the two.

Yet, perfect mutual understanding is not what is required. Perhaps it is enough to spend time together in one another's modes of enquiry, and then to allow the science to continue, and the writing to continue; each somehow touched by the other, each somehow knowing more of the other, and each secure in its own status as a knowledge production system that works to make sense of existence.

Biographies

Invited Scientist

Tokoloho Rampai is a senior lecturer in the Department of Chemical Engineering, University of Cape Town (UCT). She was a PhD qualifier through Wits University 2020. She has 15 years of collective experience in academia and research. She is one of the founding members of Marine and Antarctic Research for Innovation and Sustainability (MARIS) at UCT, which is a large cross-faculty multidisciplinary research centre. Within MARIS, she manages the Innovation in Chemical, Materials and Observational Engineering discipline portfolio in the Scientific Steering Committee, in addition to being director of MARIS@CHE.

Her research focus is mainly materials engineering, this is applied both in Antarctic sea ice research and advanced ceramic materials development for application in catalytic processes. In advanced ceramics research, she focuses on powder metallurgy, thermodynamics for materials development, material properties evaluation and tribological testing for suitability of application. And in sea ice research, she focuses on improving understanding of the dynamics of sea ice growth and how this gives rise to the material properties (microstructure and mechanics) of Antarctic sea ice. This is predominantly carried out through artificial sea ice growth experiments in temperature-controlled laboratory conditions and nominally through field testing in the marginal ice zone in the Southern Ocean.

She is an active supervisor of postgraduate students and has published in sea ice, engineering, and ceramics development journals. In 2021, she joined the Association of Polar Early Career Scientists in South Africa (APECSSA) where she conceptualised, initiated and managed the mentorship portfolio which was successfully transferred to SAPRI (South African Polar Research Infrastructure) in 2023 as a national initiative. In 2022 she became an associate member of the Scientific Committee on Oceanic Research (SCOR) Working Group: Meltwater Stratification. And in 2024 was nominated for membership in the South African National Committee for the Scientific Committee for Antarctic Research (SANC for SCAR). Within this committee she is co-manager of the Physical Sciences group and Instabilities & Thresholds in Antarctica (INSTANT) portfolio.

Writers

Boitumelo (Tumi) Riet is a theatremaker, poet, performer, arts entrepreneur, story doula and an emerging cultural worker. She is a multipurposed creative with an acute skill in devising, making performance theatre, creating and opening spaces where stories are shared. Her artistic statement is, "I create counterpoisons". This is a theme that is visible throughout the radical and fresh creative works she offers and that she is part of. Recently she has opened a storytelling platform called Unwinding Your Knots, where she offers space and guides people to share personal stories in creative and embodied ways.

Her passion lies in various forms of storytelling and expression—particularly in relation to her communities and herself. Performance, writing, poetry and the visual arts are some of the ways she uses to reach, impact and understand the society she inhabits. Her approach to creation is centred in interrogation of the physical and metaphysical realities around and beyond her, and how she can constructively affect them. This is always a golden thread visible in her artistic produce. Tumi has a bold, authentic and radical voice, and it is with this voice that she launched a project that aims to decentralise the arts in Bloemfontein, Free State, called Bantu Tales: Ditlhamane Tsa Gae. She ultimately believes in the holistic practice of storytelling being brought closer to home, into our friendship and familial groups, but most importantly in the communities of South Africa.

Campbell Meas is an actress, writer, director, facilitator, experimental film enthusiast and theatre maker. Graduating from Wits University with a BADA Honours in Performance and Directing, as well as graduating with Performance training from Indigo view Academy in 2016 she has been a part of theatre groups, The Movement RSA and Jittery Citizens, performing in a variety of award winning shows, most notably the Naledi-winning *Just Antigone*. She has been afforded the opportunity to work within the film and theatre industry in various roles over the years, garnering much experience on stage, in front and behind the camera. Moving into the teaching space she has lectured and taught at both Wits university as well as the Market theatre lab from 2018 to present. As part of her writing collective, she has received two NAC grants to write, produce and shoot a TV pilot dealing with mental health and adulthood. Having been a CASA playwright finalist a few years back, she is also the winner of the 2025 National Arts Festival playwright competition under Heineken, staging her original work *VAKAVIGWA* at this year's fest. Her own projects deal with intimate stories that also push mediums to new creative spaces.

David Cornwell is the author of the novels *Like It Matters* (2016), which was shortlisted for the Etisalat Prize for Best African Debut Novel, and *Hell of a Country* (August 2025 from Kwela Books), a fictionalised retelling of the infamous Scissors Murder from the 1970s. He has also written a play, *White Elephant* (staged in 2017), and he is the co-writer and co-producer of *Pou* (Peacock), an award-winning Gothic horror film starring Tarryn Wyngaard and Johan Botha (released on Amazon Prime in 2021). He writes songs and plays guitar in a duo with Danieyella Rodin, having previously played in bands like Sixgun Gospel and KRAAL. He is currently working on a short-form science fiction project, Orphan Data, and his third novel, an intergenerational family saga called Poor White Spiritual. He is a graduate of the University of Cape Town's Master's in Creative Writing programme (2011), where his collection of short stories (*Yet Trouble Came*) was supervised by Damon Galgut.

Efemia Chela. I am a Zambian-Ghanaian writer who was nominated for the Caine Prize for African Writing in 2014 and shortlisted for the Gerald Kraak Prize in 2017. My short stories have been published in places such as *Wasafiri*, *New Internationalist*, *Short Story Day Africa* anthologies, *Brittle Paper*, and *PEN Passages: Africa*. I am currently at work on my debut novel and represented by Pontas.

Emile Conje. I am a storyteller and architect. After graduating in 2013, my experience in the world of so-called 'development' created a deep discomfort in me with the way we see and understand our human position in relation to each other and other living things. I subsequently stepped away from the industry and turned to stories and poetry to help understand and heal the rift and imbalance I experience in so many day-to-day interactions: discarding without consideration, expecting compliance with oppressive systems, and neglecting honest expression of our true experiences. I currently work part-time as a media analyst for HB Media and as an assistant lecturer at the Department of Architecture at the University of Pretoria. I also perform poetry and host creative writing workshops from time to time.

I have a deep interest in 'trash' and the meaning revealed by the ways we manage the resources in which we do not see value. This manifests in my ongoing writing project 'n Hoop Gemors // A Pile of Trash, as well as 'trashy' craft projects and ongoing research with colleagues at the University of Pretoria. I am currently working on a work of fiction with themes touching on death and immortality, our dependence on an intimate relationship with the Land, the fallacy of individual identity without community and how to rebuild a sense of belonging after committing the worst.

John Trengove is a South African writer and director. His debut feature, *The Wound* (*Inxeba*), opened at Sundance and in Berlin and was named "the most important LGBT film you will see in 2018" by *i-D* magazine. The controversial film was briefly banned in his home country and was shortlisted for the International Feature Oscar. His second feature, *Manodrome*, starring Jesse Eisenberg, Adrien Brody and Odessa Young, premiered in Berlin and was released internationally in 2024. John has worked extensively in television and theatre. Most recently, he directed on the Cape Town crime drama *White Lies* with Natalie Dormer, released in 2024. His limited series, *Hopeville*, won a Rose d' Or award and was nominated for an international Emmy. In 2017 he received an honorary award from South Africa's Department of Arts and Science for his work in television. His theatre work includes the cult hit *The Epicene Butcher* which played at the Edinburgh Festival. John trained as an actor and studied film at NYU's Tisch School of the Arts. He lives between Cape Town and São Paulo with his husband, filmmaker Marco Dutra.

Lee Middleton is a Korean-American creative non-fiction writer and journalist, based in Cape Town, South Africa since 2006. She is currently working on a genre-blending memoir / creative non-fiction book exploring the legacy of 70 years of transnational adoption from South Korea, and the consequences of that practice on transracial adoptees as well as Korea's child welfare system, women's rights and the country's current "depopulation crisis".

As a journalist, she began her career covering wildlife conservation in relation to local communities around the African continent. More recently, she has covered sustainable development and urbanisation (specifically issues around spatial inclusion and so-called informality in African cities). She has written for *Time Magazine, Quartz Africa,*

Cityscapes Magazine and the *Mail & Guardian*, among others. Having previously researched wild tiger populations in Thailand's national parks, fished for salmon in Alaska, and worked as a human rights observer in Chiapas, Mexico, she is an avid believer in pursuing one's instincts wherever they lead.

Linda Lee Mhlongo, also known as Mr Lee, is a performing arts graduate from Sibikwa Arts Centre, where he studied for four years, before going to the Market Theatre Laboratory, where he did short courses in creative dance, scriptwriting and directing. Lee is a qualified facilitator in arts and culture programmes and has an Advanced Teachers Certificate in Playmaking; and in 2022 he graduated at the South African Creative Industries Incubator where he did Creative Entrepreneurship. He was born in a place called Nced' Omhlophe, Engquthu, KwaZulu-Natal, and he grew up in Daveyton where he went to primary and high school.

Linda Lee began writing for audiences in high school, with a play called *Blown Minds*, which was about apartheid South Africa, and it also contained a poem of that name. He would later write a large body of poetry that was mainly used in his theatre works and drama training sessions. In 2003 he adapted Bessie Head's novel *Maru* into a playscript that was performed extensively for Grade 12 learners.

He has also written *Laf'Elihle*, the story of Cetshwayo, a Zulu king. The play was invited to be performed in China, and it was also part of many play contests, including the Market Theatre Laboratory Community Theatre Festival. Mr Lee has two unpublished works called "The Little Book of Big Poems" and "Scars of the Orphaned Thorn", a literary work of short stories, playscripts, essays and poetry.

Senna-Marie is a Johannesburg-based songwriter and interdisciplinary artist drawn to the frictions that shape intimacy. Rooted in the emotional resonance of her lyricism, her sound recalls '70s alt-folk with experimental art-pop and jazz influences.

She writes and performs in close collaboration with her friend Ryan Schultze; together they have released *Fence Sitter* (debut EP, 2021) and *Golden* (single, 2023) and are currently in-studio with their full band completing their upcoming full-length album *All of the Ants* (release date early 2026). Highlights include live performances at Nirox Arts Foundation and Black Labone Earth Day.

Senna-Marie's work extends to audiovisual experimentation where analogue projection, gesture and shadow play are interwoven with song—explored in *Square Eyes* (live video performance, 2024) and *Threshold* (music video, 2025). Her wider practice spans event cura-tion, accompaniment, musical collaborations and arts education.

Tshepo Molefe (pronouns: he/his/him) is a multi-award-winning performance poet and copywriter. With a career spanning over nine years, Molefe has graced many South African stages and has been published in numerous publications. His career highlights include being published in the seventh edition of the *Sol Plaatje Anthology*, winning the 2017 WordnSound Poetry league and publishing his debut poetry anthology, *The Brown Bottle Series*.

Yuwinn Kraukamp. I'm a writer from a coastal corner of South Africa where small towns still exist. I'm a booklover, a natural born creative and a patron (saint) of everything that's artistically unique and beautifully weird in this world. My writing skillset is a fusion of creative intelligence and linguistic acuity, a product of my academic background in literature and language studies. In the past four years I have worked as a journalist, columnist, short-story writer and occasional poet. My writing capabilities have been practised, proven and published numerous times across several mediums, diverse genres and in multiple languages. This includes three magazines, three newspapers, two anthologies, and more.

My humble list of accomplishments includes winning the Department of Education's radio drama contest in 2022, a writing accomplishment in Los Angeles, California, for the Feminist Futures

Award, as well as being selected one of Toyin Falola's top 25 African writers (in October 2022). I'm a life-long believer in the beauty and timelessness of words; that the right words written with a bit of magic can absolutely change a reader's entire world. All in all, I'm completely devoted to honing my craft (on all levels) to become the best writer I can be in this lifetime.

Editors

Mehita Iqani is an academic researcher and writer in the field of media, communications and cultural studies, in which she has published widely. She is currently the director of the Centre for Science Communication, based in the Journalism Department at Stellenbosch University, where she runs research projects on climate and environment, health and happiness, and creative communications through the DSI-NRF-funded SA Research Chair in Science Communication, of which she is Chairholder.

Wamuwi Mbao is a writer and literary critic. He teaches literature at Stellenbosch University. His research interests are in South African popular culture, literary criticism, mid-century modern architecture, and automotive histories. He is the editor of *Years of Fire and Ash: South African Poetry of Decolonization*. He is a fiction critic with the *Johannesburg Review of Books*. His work has appeared in various publications. His short story 'The Bath' was noted as one of the most significant short stories of South Africa's new democracy. He is the recipient of a South African Literary Award for his body of literary criticism.

www.ingramcontent.com/pod-product-compliance
Lightning Source LLC
Chambersburg PA
CBHW070351270326
41926CB00017B/4092